THINGS TO DO IN PHOENIX BEFORE YOU DIE

100 THINGS TO DO IN PHOENIX BEFORE YOU DIE

CHRISTINE K. BAILEY

Reedy Press
PO Box 5131
St. Louis, MO 63139, USA
www.reedypress.com

Library of Congress Control Number: 2015942720

ISBN: 9781681060170

Design by Jill Halpin

Printed in the United States of America
15 16 17 18 19   5 4 3 2 1

Please note that websites, phone numbers, addresses, and company names are subject to change or cancellation. We did our best to relay the most accurate information available, but due to circumstances beyond our control, please do not hold us liable for misinformation. When exploring new destinations, please do your homework before you go.

CONTENTS

PREFACE

There are countless lists of things to see and do in Phoenix and the surrounding areas, or, as the locals call it, "the Valley of the Sun" or "the Valley" for short. And most are chock full of things you want to add to your to-do list. After all, located in the very heart of the Sonoran Desert, Phoenix is a remarkable gateway where the Wild West and the twenty-first century meet in a blend of cowboy culture, Mexican and Native American influences, and a certain pioneering spirit all evolving into a decidedly urban landscape. Since this is a list of 100 things to do before you die, I've focused on the very best of these elements as well as one of the area's greatest attractions—the beautiful weather and breathtaking desert landscape. In fact, climate is considered one of the five C's that built the state's economy along with cattle, citrus, cotton, and copper. It's still one of the biggest reasons more than sixteen million people visit the Phoenix area each year, and may very well be the reason you're here. The truth is, you can shop anywhere, listen to music anywhere, and eat great food in any metropolitan city. But the desert weather and scenic landscape can transform even the most mundane activity into something worth repeating. This list focuses on the very best of the best the area has to offer. Discover, explore, learn something new, and enjoy the adventure!

HOW OTHERS SEE US

It has been aptly speculated that the reason Phoenix, Arizona, is called Phoenix is that every summer the city burns to ashes in the heat and they have to rebuild it.

"Arizona is gorgeous. The sunshine in Arizona is gorgeous red."

—Cecilia Bartoli, author

"Arizona, our beautiful state, was built on mining."

—Jan Brewer, author and former governor of Arizona

"Welcome to Arizona, where summer spends the winter—and hell spends the summer."

—popular saying, modified from a booster slogan in the 1930s

"You know you're an Arizona native when you take rain dances seriously."

—Skip Boyer, quoted in *You Know You're an Arizona Native, When . . .*, compiled by Don Dedera, 1993

"My favorite color . . . the seam of a desert horizon."

—Eileen Tabios

"You know you live in Phoenix when the cold-water faucet is hotter than the hot-water faucet."

—author unknown

DEDICATION

This book is dedicated to those with a pioneering spirit—both in our past and today—who set out to discover the new frontier. Travel fulfills that very human need to learn and explore. Today, while it may seem that all corners of the earth have been discovered and surveyed, there are still spaces and places new to each of us—ready to inspire and transform us should we have the courage to step out our own front doors.

FOOD AND DRINK

1

DINE DOWN
IN THE BARRIO AT BARRIO CAFE

When you think of Arizona and the Southwest, tasty Mexican food often comes to mind. But the great thing about Arizona's Mexican cuisine is that it's not just "traditional" Tex-Mex influence you'll find in these palatable dishes. You'll also find an infusion of New Mexican and Native American recipes and ingredients, as well as the influences of specific provinces within Mexico—like the Sonora Mexican twist you'll find at Chef Silvana Salcido Esparza's Cafe Barrio. Located in South Phoenix, Cafe Barrio serves up dishes you may not recognize, but will instantly fall in love with after one bite, like *chiles en nogada*—a delightful mix of cheese, nuts, fruit, and chicken stuffed into poblano peppers. This mouthwatering culinary concoction will make your taste buds sing. Pair it with a margarita on the rocks.

2814 N 16th St., Phoenix, AZ 85004, 602-636-0240
Barriocafe.com

2

FEAST
ON FOOD TRUCK FRIDAYS

The Phoenix Street Food Coalition is more than sixty food trucks strong and offers something to please just about every palate, from hot dogs to seafood and everything in between—including dessert trucks like Frosted Frenzy Cupcakes and Mamma Toledo's Pies (fruit pies, chocolate pies, custard pies, and more). For one of the best roundups in town, check out the parking lot at Central and McKinley every Friday from 11 a.m. to 1:30 p.m. Depending on the Friday, you may discover local favorites like Short Leash Hot Dog's quirky take on the great American frankfurter (no buns, just naan and ingredients like bacon, jalapenos, and peanut butter), the Lobster Lady's lobster rolls (yes, tasty as can be in the middle of the Sonoran Desert), and Emerson Fry Bread (a must-try since fry bread is a Native American delicacy here in Arizona).

721 N Central Ave., Phoenix, AZ 85004
phxstreetfood.org
http://phxstreetfood.org/truck-directory

TIP
For a daily list of which food trucks will be where, try their Facebook page—www.facebook.com/phxstreetfood.

3

DIG INTO THE BEST PIZZA
IN THE SOUTHWEST

With a high percentage of Arizona's transplants from pizza capitals like New York, New Jersey, and Chicago, it's no surprise that they would bring their favorite dish along with them, or that they would be such a demanding bunch. Phoenicians get to enjoy the spoils of this battle as local chefs try to outdo one another with their signature pies. While there are local favorites like the Chicago-style deep dish at Oregano's and trendy California-style pizzas at La Grande Orange Pizzeria, the crowning achievement to date has been Chris Bianco's brick-oven-baked, thin-crust pizza made with the freshest ingredients (like fresh basil, smoked mozzarella, and locally grown veggies) at Pizzeria Bianco located in Phoenix Science and Heritage Park in downtown Phoenix. This local gem has been an inspiration that has spawned a whole line of Italian-influenced pies that will make you reconsider all of your pizza allegiances.

Pizzeriabianco.com

TIP

Chef Chris Bianco has four Phoenix-based restaurants: Pizzeria Bianco (downtown), Bar Bianco (wine bar adjaent to the downtown pizzeria), Pane Bianco (made-to-order brick-oven-baked bread and sandwiches on Central Avenue), and the latest Pizzeria Bianco, which opened up at 22nd Street and Camelback. So if you don't want to stand in line at the original downtown location just to get your name on the waiting list, consider trying one of his other restaurants. The wait may be significantly less; but the food is just as delicious.

Downtown
Pizzeria Bianco & Bar Bianco
623 E Adams St., Phoenix, AZ 85004, 602-258-8300

Pizzeria Bianco Town & Country
4743 N 20th St., Phoenix, AZ 85016, 602-368-3273

Pane Bianco
4404 N Central Ave., Phoenix, AZ 85012

SIP AN UMBRELLA DRINK POOLSIDE

AT ONE OF THE RESORT POOLS

There's something to be said about sipping an umbrella drink beside the clear sparkling waters of one of the Valley's resorts, and there are so many to choose from. Take the party atmosphere of Hotel Valley Ho in Scottsdale, the Vegas-size mega-pools of the Fairmount Princess or the Phoenician, the historic pool at the Arizona Biltmore (beside which Irving Berlin penned "White Christmas"), the pool set high above the desert floor against Pinnacle Peak at the Four Seasons Resort Scottsdale at Troon North, and the quiet oasis at the Royal Palms to name only a few. Each of the area's resorts offer impeccably crafted cocktails. So grab one of those luxurious lounge chairs, slather on some sun screen, put your feet up, and call for your waiter.

5

SEE 360-DEGREE DESERT VIEWS

AT COMPASS ARIZONA GRILL

The 2014 winner of OpenTable Diners' Choice Awards for Top 100 Scenic View Restaurants in America, the Compass Arizona Grill in the Hyatt Regency tower sits high above the desert floor in the center of downtown Phoenix. The rotating restaurant offers 360-degree views of the sprawling city below and the desert beyond. You'll also see natural landmarks within the city limits such as Camelback Mountain, Piestewa Peak, and Phoenix South Mountain Preserve, and distant iconic mountain ranges like Four Peaks, White Tank Mountains, and Superstition Mountains. For the best view, sit in one of the booths for dinner; the menu covers an eclectic mix of Southwestern fare. Or stop in at the lounge after a Diamondback baseball game or Phoenix Suns basketball game for late-night happy hour prices.

Hyatt Regency Phoenix
122 North Second St., Phoenix, AZ 85004, 602-252-123
Compassarizona.com

DINE RAT-PACK STYLE
AT DURANT'S

Harken back to another era at Durant's. A Valley staple for more than sixty years, Durant's is a throwback to the Rat Pack era of Phoenix when the city's population topped out at significantly less than half a million. Durant's hasn't changed all that much—you'll still find the same deep red wallpaper and dark red leather booths—but it hasn't needed to; it still serves some of the best steak in the city and provides flawless service to its patrons. The menu includes traditional steak house favorites like prime rib at steak house sizes. You'll also find delicious salads like the Cobb. Save room for dessert: consider the strawberry shortcake for two (so big it's more like "for four," but yummy nonetheless).

Durantsaz.com

TIP

Don't enter through the front door. In fact, most locals don't know there's a front door, let alone where they might find it. Instead, park in the back and slip in through the kitchen door, where you'll make your way past the friendly cooking and wait staff into the back hallway of the restaurant. In keeping with its bygone-era persona, Durant's has a strict no-cellphone policy, so you may want to keep your phone in your pocket.

2611 North Central Avenue, Phoenix, AZ 85004
602-264-5967

EAT THE BEST
NEW MEXICAN CUISINE IN ARIZONA AT RICHARDSON'S

This may be Arizona, but you'll find a number of restaurants serving New Mexico–style cuisine and Richardson's may very well be the best of the best. Owned by Richardson Browne, Richardson's has been serving the Valley New Mexican–influenced steak and seafood dishes since 1988. Add to the heavily influenced menu, the dark, low-lit interior, wooden beams, and adobe walls and you won't find a better Santa Fe–style dining experience anywhere else in the Valley. The menu here incorporates both green and red chilies and the food is spicy-hot so order with care. Try the New Mexican platter off the menu, which will give you a variety to sample, including the cheese *relleno* (cheese stuffed pepper), chicken *burro* (aka a burrito), and bacon-wrapped shrimp, or you can try the *carne adovada* (smoked pork slowly cooked in red chile sauce). Also the fresh tamales and green chile potatoes are local favorites.

6335 North 16th St., Phoenix, AZ 85016, 602-265-5886

TIP

Visit Dick's Hideaway across the street and down the way along 16th Street for a quick taste of the Santa Fe Trail and a drink at this little bar. 6008 N 16th St., Phoenix, AZ 85016, 602-241-1881

8

TREAT YOURSELF
TO DINNER AT THE BEST FRENCH RESTAURANT IN THE VALLEY

The Valley's number one French restaurant for more than five years in a row, *Coup des Tartes,* is one of the Valley's many gems. Booted from their original location after more than fifteen years, *Coup des Tartes* rallied and found an even better spot at 17th Street and Osborn. The restaurant's intimate setting is reminiscent of private dining in a friend's home, and the seasonal menu and evolving dessert tray keep locals coming back for more. On the menu you'll find cheese and charcuterie plates vying for your attention with appetizers like the savory three onion *tarte* or the *escargot persillade* and of course the equally delicious, but much lighter, garden salads. The dinner menu covers the gamut with choices like seared sea scallops, maple leaf duck breast, and beef tenderloin. If you find you've arrived early, slip into the little bar to the left of the hostess desk for one of their garden-inspired cocktails.

1725 E Osborn Rd., Phoenix, AZ 85016, 602-212-1082
Nicetartes.com

9

SAVOR
THE HONEY VANILLA LATTE AT GIANT COFFEE

Another success of local restaurateur Matt Poole of Matt's Big Breakfast, Giant Coffee has created a creamy concoction of coffee, honey, and milk. This honey vanilla latte is shaken, not stirred, so as to beautifully blend all of these delicious ingredients. Add a homemade treat like the baker's favorite, which is a light, buttery croissant; Giant Coffee's take on the chocolate chip cookie with little bits of toffee baked in; or their Giant-sized biscotti (almost a foot of almond anise–flavored crunchy goodness). Find a seat in front of the floor-to-ceiling windows that look out over the inspiring Cancer Survivors Park on 1st Street. Most of the year these windows are pulled back, creating an open air space to relax and enjoy your latte and maybe a book or a conversation with a friend—an ideal opportunity to enjoy the desert weather.

Giantcoffeeaz.com

TIP

Giant Coffee is a short walk from the Phoenix Art Museum on Central.

DESIGN A DONUT
AT FRACTURED PRUNE DOUGHNUTS

Maybe you've already seen one of these delightful little donut factories; they seem to be popping up all over the Valley. If you have, you know you're going back for more. If not, you'll want to stop by this one-of-a-kind donut concept that's sort of like a build-a-bear workshop, but for donuts. According to DowntownTempe.com, there are more than 155,000 different variations of the donut to be had at the Fractured Prune. These delicious fried delicacies are made to order with your choice of nineteen glazes and thirteen toppings. You're sure to find your favorite. One clever customer blended sweet and savory into an amazingly scrumptious bacon, sugar, maple-glazed donut. So good, they may have to put it in the donut hall of fame.

521 S College Ave., Unit 112, Tempe, AZ 85281, 480-556-1090
Fracturedprune.com

11

QUENCH YOUR THIRST
AT A LOCAL LANDMARK

A local landmark, Four Peaks Brewery on 8th Street is located in a historic, late nineteenth-century building that was once a creamery. Just southeast of ASU's Tempe campus, with both indoor and outdoor patio seating, there are any number of flavorsome dishes at this local brewery and brew pub. For a taste of the Southwest, order the *carne adovada*, and add the two eggs over easy. The cherry wood–smoked red chile pork may very well melt in your mouth. Add the stoutamisu for dessert. This Four Peaks version of tiramisu means these lady fingers are soaked in the brewery's Oatmeal Stout. The entire menu is delicious—from the juicy Southwest burger to the 8th Street Pale Ale–battered chicken strips. Locals have their favorite brews; the most prevalent would be Kiltlifter, and for a truly local flavor try the Arizona Peach Ale.

1340 E 8th St., Suite 104, Tempe, AZ 85281, 480-303-9967
15745 N Hayden Rd., Scottsdale, AZ 85260, 480-991-1795
Fourpeaks.com

TIP

Schedule a tour before you dine and get a firsthand look at the brewery (and a chance to sample the beer before you order).

TAKE A CULINARY JOURNEY

THROUGH THE DESERT AT ARIZONA'S ONLY AAA FIVE-DIAMOND RESTAURANT

The Pima word for "seed"—*kai*—highlights the best of the Southwest in a fine-dining experience unequaled anywhere else in the state. Kai is on the property of the Wild Horse Pass Resort and Spa on the Gila River Indian Community—home to the Pima and Maricopa Indians. The tantalizing menu showcases ingredients of the Sonoran Desert and incorporates produce from Gila River Farms. One of the best ways to experience that journey is through the seven- and thirteen-course tasting menus. From palate-cleansing amuse-bouche to the grand finale dessert, each course will bring you one step further along an epicurean tour of the Southwest. If you're planning on the tasting menu, be sure your entire table places the tasting menu order before 8 p.m. Reservations recommended. Note that Kai closes every summer from July through late August.

5594 W Wild Horse Pass Blvd., Chandler, AZ 85226, 602-225-0100
www.wildhorsepassresort.com/kai

TIP

While very few places in the Valley have a dress code, this Five-Diamond restaurant asks guests to refrain from wearing shorts, jeans, t-shirts, hats, or shorts, and no open-toe sandals for men.

13

ROAST S'MORES
AT FIRESKY RESORT & SPA

One of the coziest and most intimate resorts in Scottsdale is the FireSky Resort & Spa. Located just north of the downtown shopping, dining, arts, and entertainment district, this Kimpton-brand hotel prides itself on creating a home away from home. Family-friendly and pet-friendly, this resort's inner courtyard is a little oasis in the desert. Towering palm trees, flowering bougainvillea, a sandy beach–entry pool, tranquil lagoon, and two fire pits are surrounded by comfy chairs and lounge seating inviting guests to sit and relax. Once the sun sets and the desert begins to cool, FireSky staff light the fire pits, creating a campfire atmosphere just perfect for roasting marshmallows. And you won't be disappointed: grab a s'mores kit from the front desk, and settle in for a pleasant evening beneath the stars.

4925 N Scottsdale Rd., Scottsdale, AZ 85251, 480-945-7666
FireSkyresort.com

TIP

S'mores kits are complimentary and available from the front desk upon request. You can also pick up roasting sticks for your marshmallows.

GRAB SOME GRUB

AT LAST DROP BAR AT LON'S AT THE HERMOSA

Once the home of Arizona cowboy artist Lon Megargee, the property now boasts the Hermosa Inn, LON's at the Hermosa, and the Last Drop Bar. A taste of the Southwest, LON's and Last Drop serve up gourmet, cowboy-style, mouthwatering food and drinks made with fresh, locally grown ingredients like delectable pork belly tacos on house-made tortillas with pickled onions and cilantro crema or the smoky Mesquite Sour made with High West Campfire Whisky, mesquite amber syrup, lemon, egg white, and mole bitters. Find an equally delicious and expanded menu at LON's. Dine outside in spring or fall for the full Arizona dining experience: Camelback Mountain, the setting sun, a lush colorful garden, pork roasting on the spit, live music, and beautiful weather.

5532 N Palo Cristi Rd., Paradise Valley, AZ 85253, 602-955-8614
Hermosainn.com

15

TASTE THE RAINBOW
AT THE PHOENIX PUBLIC MARKET CAFE

What originally was a weekly, open-air public farmers' market in 2005 has morphed into the permanent space that now makes up at the Phoenix Public Market Cafe. The full-blown restaurant prides itself on serving stunningly perfect dishes made with seasonal, locally grown ingredients from some of the area's most fruitful farms and gardens including Maya's Farm. Dig into the most colorful salad you'll ever find called Eat the Rainbow—gluten-free, vegan-friendly, and dairy-free. This vibrant concoction served in a giant salad bowl changes seasonally and uses the area's best in-season veggies served marinated, steamed, and raw with three dipping sauces. The list of pleasing dishes here will cover you for breakfast, lunch, and dinner including the fried chicken, pork *chile verde* pot pie, the flanched flarney garney, and the surprisingly delicious chick pea pancakes served with bananas, pecans, and agave syrup.

14 E Pierce St., Phoenix, AZ 85004, 602-253-2700
Phxpublicmarket.com

16

STOP IN FOR GRIDDLECAKES

AT MATT'S BIG BREAKFAST

Hands down, the best breakfast in town is Matt's Big Breakfast. On weekends, finding a seat is next to impossible and that's in the restaurant's expanded location at First and Garfield in downtown Phoenix. Don't get distracted by the delicious-sounding specials they'll have posted on the giant chalkboard at the back of the restaurant. Stay focused on what will be the best buttermilk pancakes you have ever had, anywhere. Mom's won't even come close to these perfect golden circles, orb of butter, and silky maple syrup. Add a side of bacon delivered direct from the Pork Shop of Queen Creek. Before you take a bite, note that this bacon is so good it will ruin your palate for all other bacon. One word for all of that heavenly goodness—yum.

825 N 1st St., Phoenix, AZ 85004, 602-254-1074
mattsbigbreakfast.com

TIP

Can't make it to the downtown Phoenix location of this Guy Fieri–featured diner? Make it a point to stop in at their location at Southwest's Airport Terminal 4 on your way out of town.

17

TAKE THE OLIVE OIL TOUR
AT QUEEN CREEK OLIVE MILL

Yes, there is an olive mill on the outskirts of the Phoenix suburbs. What started out as a hobby for one family of Detroit transplants is now a thriving olive farm and mill, restaurant, and distributor of its extra virgin olive oil (EVOO) to countless stores and restaurants throughout the Arizona culinary community. Take the thirty-minute Olive Oil 101 Tour to gain interesting insight into the valuable properties of EVOO. Wrap it up with a late lunch at the farm's cafe. Try the vanilla bean olive oil waffles with whipped cream and maple syrup. While you're there, browse the store's shelves: you'll discover interesting olive oils like Mexican lime, fresh crush basil olive oil, and the vanilla bean olive oil used to make those fluffy waffles.

25062 S Meridian Rd., Queen Creek, AZ, 480-888-9290
Queencreekolivemill.com

TIP

Build in at least a few minutes to browse the store where you'll find countless gifts for others or yourself including olive oils, stuffed olives, tapenades, soaps, lip balms, bath and body oils, and cookbooks.

TOUR
THE FAMILY-OWNED CERRETA CANDY COMPANY

Located in historic downtown Glendale, the Cerreta Candy Company has been an Arizona legend in chocolate making for more than forty years. Known for delicious favorites like Cerreta's famous French mint, this is still a family business for the fourth-generation Cerreta candymakers. Tour the factory for a look at where the chocolatey magic happens. Discover how they turn ingredients like pallets of sugar and ten-pound bars of chocolate into silken curtains of melted goodness to be draped over creamy white centers or jumbo strawberries and molded into giant chocolate Santas weighing five hundred pounds. Or how that golden sea of caramel turns into a mouthwatering treat. The thirty-minute tour takes place twice daily at 10 a.m. and 1 p.m. Stop at the factory store on your way out and grab some chocolate to go.

5345 W Glendale Ave., Glendale, AZ 85301, 623-930-9000
Cerreta.com

19

STEP DOWN
INTO THE SALT CELLAR FOR SEAFOOD

The Salt Cellar in south Scottsdale has been flying their fresh fish in daily for decades. The seemingly unremarkable cream-colored building with blue awnings at the corner of Hayden Road and Pierce Street just north of McKellips is actually just a part of the award-winning seafood restaurant. Three flights of wooden stairs lead deep below ground to a tiny bar and hidden space serving some of the best fresh fish and steaks in the Valley. Pick your fresh lobster from the tank at the foot of the stairs, or pick surf and/or turf from their massive menu. Depending on the season, you'll find fish flown in from places like Hawaii, Alaska, Georges Bank, Boston, the Gulf of Mexico, and even New Zealand.

550 N Hayden Rd., Scottsdale, AZ 85257, 480-947-1963
Saltcellarrestaurant.com

TIP

Locals love the shrimp San Remo and the crab cakes appetizers. Stop in at the tiny bar for happy hour 4 to 7 p.m. and reverse happy hour from 10 p.m. 'til close.

LUNCH AT T. COOK'S
IN THE SHADOW OF CAMELBACK MOUNTAIN

If you're looking for the ladies-(or gentlemen)-who-lunch dining experience, make reservations for a leisurely lunch at T. Cook's at the Royal Palms Resort & Spa. The entire experience—from the drive through the resort's main entrance to the walk through what was once the lush inner courtyard of a private estate—offers a stunning panorama of Mediterranean-inspired architecture and beautiful gardens set against the Sonoran Desert and Camelback Mountain. T. Cook's itself is located in what was originally the Cooke Mansion. Its Saltillo tiled floors, heavy wood frames, beamed ceilings, and stunning décor make for an ideal lunch setting. The patio, located off the main dining room, is nestled against picturesque Camelback Mountain, which makes it the perfect Arizona-style setting for any occasion. The lunch menu is as spectacular and memorable as the view.

5200 E Camelback Rd., Phoenix, AZ 85018, 602-840-3610
Tcooksphoenix.com

TIP

Patio seating is first come, first served, but is worth the wait as long as it's not the middle of summer.

At night, the resort is beautifully lit with colorful twinkle lights, fire pits, and garden up-lighting and makes for a beautiful setting for a romantic evening. Talk to the resort's romance consultant about how to make your stay and your special occasion extraordinary.

Pink Jeep Tours
76

ARIZONA ADVENTURES AND SIDE TRIPS

21

GO OFF-ROADING
WITH GREEN ZEBRA TOURS

This off-road experience is especially entertaining when you're taking the dirt hills that pepper the Yavapai Reservation at top speed and splashing through mud puddles. This guided tour puts you behind the wheel of a special military-grade all-terrain vehicle (or ATV) known as a Tomcar. You'll discover more than just your penchant for white-knuckling it across the desert as you follow your guide across the desert landscape in the McDowell Mountains. Your guide will point out the history of the area, the lay of the land, and the hidden gems (like an eagle's nest high above the river).

7500 E Doubletree Ranch Rd., Scottsdale, AZ 85258, 480-629-6262
Gogreenzebra.com/Scottsdale

TIP

Be sure to bring money to tip your guide. He (or she) will have earned it.

22

HIKE, SLIDE, SWIM, CLIMB, AND RAPPEL

YOUR WAY THROUGH SALOME CANYON

So what is canyoneering? Something to do with a canyon, you might assume, and you would be correct. This 360 Adventures tour takes you on a daring trip between the towering granite walls of Salome Canyon where you'll be challenged to scramble over giant boulders, swim across bottomless pools, slide down slippery rockslides, hike sandy stretches, climb the face of rock cliffs, and rappel down the face of a twenty-five-foot waterfall to get from one end of the canyon to the other. The motto is, "the only way out is through." If the thought of this has you grinning from ear to ear with excitement, consider booking their Slippery When Wet tour in late spring when the water is still flowing from Payson to the north and hovering at a balmy seventy degrees.

Phoenix, AZ, 480-722-0360
360-adventures.com

23

WATCH THE ARIZONA SUNSET

FROM RUSTLER'S ROOSTE AT SOUTH MOUNTAIN

There's something simply breathtaking about an Arizona sunset, and you'll want to relax and savor it. Rustler's Rooste Steakhouse in South Phoenix offers one of the best places to watch the sun play out its last moments across the Valley. You'll discover why as the shadows lengthen and the colors shift across the myriad mountain ranges in the distance. Add the lights of the airplanes flying into and out of Sky Harbor International Airport and the cars speeding along the highways below, and you're in for a kaleidoscope of colors as the sun dips below the western horizon and the city lights up. Rustler's Rooste is open daily for dinner and live country music.

8383 S 48th St., Phoenix, AZ 85044, 602-431-6474
Rustlersrooste.com

TIP

For the best views, ask for patio seating or the tables by the windows.

24

EXPLORE THE DESERT
AT NIGHT AT THE DESERT BOTANICAL GARDEN

Take the flashlight tour at the Desert Botanical Garden. This self-guided sensory adventure lets you stroll along the garden paths from station to station discovering the desert's mysterious flora and fauna that come out only at night. Bring your own flashlight or purchase one at the Garden Shop. Depending on the time of year and what's out or in bloom, you may find night-blooming desert flowers like Arizona's state flower—the saguaro blossom, which only opens at night—or desert critters like tarantulas, lizards, owls, and bats. At night the desert cools and the area comes alive. Listen for and learn the unique sounds the desert makes as it comes alive after the sun sets and the stars appear in the night sky.

1201 N Galvin Pkwy., Phoenix, AZ 85008, 480-941-1225
www.dbg.org

ENJOY BEER AND BIRDS
AT NINA MASON PULLIAM RIO SALADO AUDUBON CENTER

Dedicated to introducing urbanites to the nature around them, the Nina Mason Pulliam Rio Salado Audubon Center, located along the banks of the Salt River in central Phoenix, hosts a variety of events and workshops. One of its most distinctive and ingenuous attempts to inspire city dwellers to discover the desert may be its blend of educational talk and happy hour known as Birds 'n Beer. Every third Thursday of the month from 5:30 p.m. to 7:30 p.m. locals (and tourists) can grab a beer and take a seat to learn a little more about the six-hundred-acre Rio Salado Habitat Restoration Area smack dab in the middle of their city and the more than two hundred creatures that also make central Phoenix their home. Beers are provided by local favorite Four Peaks Brewery, of course.

3131 S Central Ave., Phoenix, AZ 85040, 602-468-6470
Riosalado.audubon.org

EXPLORE
ARIZONA'S WINE COUNTRY

While Arizona has not always been synonymous with wine, lately the increasing quality of its wines has started to create national buzz and, along with it, a growing community of talented and knowledgeable grape growers and winemakers. Primarily focused in three specific areas—the Verde Valley area north of Phoenix, Sonoita, and Willcox south of Tucson—there are a number of master growers and winemakers showcasing the fruits of their labor, including a couple of winemakers in the Phoenix area. The Verde Valley is only a short drive north of the city on I-17 where you'll find a handful of vineyards and cellars, many with tasting rooms in and around Cottonwood, Jerome, Williams, and Cornville.

17235 N 75th Ave., Glendale, AZ 85308, 623-236-2338
www.ArizonaWine.org

TIP
For great information about wine in Arizona, see the Arizona Wine Growers Association website at ArizonaWine.org. You can find a list of all the wine growers and vineyards by area as well as contact information for each one.

WATCH THE SUN RISE
ABOVE THE DESERT FLOOR FROM A HOT AIR BALLOON

Clear blue skies, sun-filled days, and wide-open spaces make the Valley of the Sun an ideal place for a hot air balloon ride. Driving along I-17 on early mornings, you can see the colorful balloons drifting across the panorama of blue expanse and jagged mountain peaks. In Phoenix, you'll find countless moments that take your breath away, and the sun slowly rising up over the mountain ranges along the eastern edge of the city, the colors shifting, and the light seeping across the horizon, are some of them. The clean, crisp air and the whole valley unfurling at your feet as you rise up above it offers a 360-degree view you won't find anywhere else, no matter how high you can hike.

1725 W Williams Dr., #39, Phoenix, AZ, 480-299-0154
Rainbow Ryders.com

2243 E Rose Garden Loop, Phoenix, AZ, 480-502-6999
HotAirExpeditions.com

TIP

Despite the fact that not even the best cameras can capture the breathtaking view you'll see, don't forget to bring it anyway. You'll want to capture the moment.

PLAY CHICKEN
ON THE RED ROCKS

Arizona offers limitless visual gems, one of which is Sedona. Located about 115 miles north of Phoenix, Sedona has been named the most beautiful place in the U.S. by *USA Weekend*. One look at the rich combination of fire-red rocks, green high-desert vegetation, and expansive blue skies, and you'll understand (your soul may actually sigh). While there are a number of ways to soak up these remarkable views, from hiking to helicopter rides to simply sitting on the outdoor patio at Canyon Breeze, there's one more adventurous than the others: Pink Jeep's Broken Arrow tour. The two-hour tour, in one of those pink jeeps you'll see all over town, takes you directly out onto the red rocks for a very wild ride.

204 State Rte. 89A, Sedona, AZ 86336, 928-203-7021
PinkJeepToursSedona.com

TIP

Take a few photos to capture the moment, but don't waste too much time behind the lens. And don't be afraid to let loose a scream or two as your very talented guide/driver teases the edges of gravity and takes that jeep right up against the sky.

29

LOSE YOURSELF
IN THE GRANDEST CANYON IN THE WORLD

It's one of the seven natural wonders of the world. The sheer numbers alone will overwhelm you: one mile deep, almost twenty miles wide in places, almost three hundred miles long (in river miles), and more than one million acres of park land. But it's the sight of all of those numbers added up into one take-your-breath-away moment when you see it all for the first time that will leave you grasping to comprehend the very awesomeness of what you're seeing. "Grand" cannot do it justice and neither can a million photos no matter their worth at a thousand words apiece. While some may say "it's just a hole in the ground," it's unlike anything you have seen or ever will see again. The Grand Canyon gives new meaning to the term awe-inspiring.

928-638-7888, nps.gov/grca

TIP

When we say lose yourself, we mean metaphorically. Be careful! Follow the signs, stay on the paths, and don't step too close to the edge. There are very few barriers or fences, so it can be as dangerous as it is beautiful.

30

HEAR THE TALE
OF THE LOST DUTCHMAN'S GOLD AT GOLDFIELD GHOST TOWN

Goldfield was a short-lived success as a gold mining town. Losing its post office only five years after it was founded in 1893, Goldfield quickly became a ghost town. The little settlement found far greater success almost one hundred years later when it was reopened as a tourist attraction in 1988. Today, Goldfield Ghost Town, set against the backdrop of the Superstition Mountains, has preserved the many legends of the area—particularly the story of the Lost Dutchman's Gold. Take the twenty-minute ride on the train as it circles town and listen as your guide shares the haunting tale of Jacob Waltz and his lost treasure. You can also pan for gold, watch a staged gunfight, and take a mine tour at this family-friendly tourist attraction.

4650 N Mammoth Mine Rd., Apache Junction, AZ 85119, 480-983-0333
Goldfieldghosttown.com

31

GO TUBING
DOWN THE SALT RIVER

The Salt River is a misnomer in the Valley. In fact, local legend has it that German POWs during World War II were quite disappointed when they tried to make a quick getaway down the Salt River and into Mexico. When they arrived, the river was but a trickle between its banks. Back at the turn of the twentieth century, the Roosevelt Dam was built to protect the city from flooding and create a series of water reservoirs, which keeps the river down to that trickle. Today, the Salt River still runs, only much farther east of the Phoenix area. It's a local tradition to float down the river in inner tubes as the river wends its way through the Tonto National Forest and Usery Mountain Park east of Phoenix.

9200 N Bush Hwy., Mesa, AZ 85215, 480-984-3305
SaltRiverTubing.com

TIP

Tubing down the Salt River is a summer treat when temps hit triple digits. Consider going with a tour company so you can take the shuttle bus back to your car—you'll end up miles from your original starting point. Depending on the trip you take (be sure to get off at the correct exit to catch your shuttle bus back), you may be on the river from one and a half hours to almost five hours. Don't bring any glass bottles; they will be confiscated before you get on the water. Do bring plenty of water; Salt River Tubing recommends one to two bottles of water per hour you expect to be on the river. Other must-haves include snacks, hats, sunscreen, closed-toe shoes, and cash only for tube rentals. Visit the tour company's website for more tips and suggestions about what to do.

TAKE A HAIR-RAISING RIDE
ALONG THE HISTORIC APACHE TRAIL

This is one road that they shouldn't ever pave. Arizona State Road 88, also known as Apache Trail and AZ88, winds its way through the Superstition Mountains from Apache Junction in the south to Roosevelt Lake at the northern end, and will take you through some of the most beautiful desert in Arizona. You'll also find the lower and upper cliff dwellings of the Salado and the historical Roosevelt Lake, completed in 1911. Start at former stagecoach stop Tortilla Flat, now a single-digit population town above Canyon Lake. Grab lunch at the lone pub—Superstition Restaurant & Saloon—before you drive your vehicle along this hair-raising, unpaved road through Arizona's backcountry. At the end, you'll come out just below the upper and lower cliff dwellings in Tonto National Park with Roosevelt Lake sparkling below.

Tonto National Monument, 26260 N. AZ Hwy. 188, Roosevelt, AZ 85545
www.nps.gov/tont

1 Main St., Tortilla Flat, AZ 85190
tortillaflataz.com/restaurant.html

TIP

The ride can be a bit nerve-wracking at times. If you get nervous navigating narrow, windy roads or you want to enjoy the scenery instead of driving, consider taking a tour with a company like Detours of Arizona. Tour drivers/guides will not only drive you along the Apache Trail, they'll also take you to a number of landmarks along the way, including Goldfield Ghost Town, Tortilla Flat, and *Dolly Steamboat* on Canyon Lake.

GO EIGHT-SECONDS

FRIDAY NIGHTS AT THE BUFFALO CHIP

Not thirty miles from central Phoenix, the Buffalo Chip Saloon & Steakhouse is where you'll find a rowdy combination of professional bull riding, live music, and an all-you-can-eat fish buffet on Friday nights. Travel back to the Old West when you step inside this massive dance hall. What was once the local feed and bait shop in Cave Creek is now a six-thousand-square-foot dance hall and saloon. Warped wooden planks, ancient cowboy boots hanging from the rafters, and riders going eight seconds on real, live bulls for a chance to win thousands of dollars will give you a taste of what once was. Belly up to the bar for a beer, twirl around the dance floor, or step outside to watch some serious bull riding.

6811 E Cave Creek Rd., Cave Creek, AZ, 480-488-9118
BuffaloChipSaloon.com

WATCH THE DESERT
COME ALIVE IN MARCH AT BOYCE THOMPSON ARBORETUM

While the Sonoran Desert only sees an average of eight inches of rain annually, the rainfall in the winter months of January, February, and March produces enough to leave the desert awash in a spectacular presentation of color in spring. This time of year, the desert is suddenly carpeted in a lush blanket of white, pink, purple, yellow, and orange blooms on flowering cacti such as the majestic saguaro and desert prickly pear, blooming trees like the foothill paloverde, and the fragrant creosote bush—most noticeable after the rain. Drive out US 60 east toward Apache Junction for a look at spring in full bloom at the Boyce Thompson Arboretum, the oldest botanical garden in Arizona, which houses plants from deserts around the world.

Boyce Thompson Arboretum SP, 37615 US Hwy. 60, 520-689-2811
Azstateparks.com/parks/both

35

HIKE
OAK CREEK CANYON'S WEST FORK TRAIL IN THE FALL

Oak Creek slips over rocks and murmurs through Oak Creek Canyon north of Sedona, leaving in its wake verdant banks of deciduous trees in the high desert of the Coconino National Forest. The West Fork Trail, which traverses the creek more than ten times as it weaves back and forth across the canyon floor, provides a delightfully cool hike in summer. The towering red rocks and trees provide ample shade and much cooler temperatures in summer, and even in spring the remnants of winter (melting piles of snow) can often be seen. But it's in fall, as summer begins to fade and the leaves begin to change, that the canyon is brimming with breathtaking color. The Oak Creek Canyon Scenic Drive north of Sedona is beautiful any time of year; however, it's particularly spectacular in fall.

431 Hwy., 179 B-1, Sedona, AZ 86336, 928-282-5820
Thehikehouse.com

TIP

The Hike House in Sedona, off 89A before you hit "the Y," provides an excellent collection of trail books, maps, and equipment. Stop in and their knowledgeable staff can point out trail options based on your preferences and physical stamina. Or visit their website for a comprehensive list of trails, directions, and what to expect. For a scenic hike of Sedona's red rocks, try the uphill hike—the Brins Mesa Trail.

TIGER SPLASH
OUT OF AFRICA

Out of Africa's Tiger Splash is a show you won't find at just any zoo or wildlife park. Carefully structured to harness the natural predator's play instincts, Tiger Splash is an exciting, fun, and often funny event where one or more of the park's Siberian and Bengal tigers jump, chase, catch, and stalk toys dragged by their caretakers (at the ends of very long sticks) in and around a shallow play pool. The show will delight and amaze you as the tigers romp across the pool, stalk one another, and interact among themselves and with their caretakers. Located about ninety minutes north of Phoenix, Out of Africa is not just about seeing the animals. It offers an interactive wildlife experience and an educational perspective about the natural behavior of the animals.

3505 W SR-260, Camp Verde, AZ 86322
OutofAfricaPark.com

TIP

Tiger Splash can be seen once a day, every day at 1:15 p.m.

TAKE A SUNRISE HORSEBACK RIDE TO YOUR BREAKFAST IN SAGUARO NATIONAL PARK

There's no better way to see the Sonoran Desert than from horseback on a morning ride through the Rincon Mountains east of Tucson. The historic Tanque Verde Ranch is a working cattle and guest ranch. Set on more than six hundred acres along the edges of Saguaro National Park and the Coronado National Forest, the ranch has more than 150 horses waiting for guests to saddle up for a morning breakfast ride through the desert. The early morning ride traverses a rocky trail that climbs steeply into the mountains (don't worry—your horse has better footing than you do). Your horse's stride is steady as the sun crests the peaks and the Saguaro cacti stand tall against the rugged terrain. Breathe in the crisp desert air; as you get closer, you'll smell bacon frying and blueberry pancakes on the griddle. Get ready for a delicious breakfast and a spectacular morning view.

14301 E Speedway Blvd,, Tucson, AZ 85748, 520-296-6275
Tanqueverderanch.com

TIP

To book individual rides, contact the ranch. Breakfast rides are Sunday and Thursday, 7:45 a.m. and 10:15 a.m., at $75/person. If you're staying at the ranch, the ride should be part of your all-inclusive package.

GLIDE
THROUGH THE PIMA AIR AND SPACE MUSEUM

Aviation fan or not, the Pima Air and Space Museum in Tucson offers a spectacular array of planes from across history and the world. The museum offers a special tribute to the US's aviation history, and passionate volunteers share facts and figures and tell the stories of the men and women who flew these aircraft. The museum sits on eighty acres and exhibits some of the most amazing feats of travel, technology, and weaponry among its more than 150 planes, including presidential planes such as JFK/LBJ Air Force One, fighter planes like the B-29 Superfortress of World War II, and the speed-and-altitude-record-holding jet—the SR-71A Blackbird— which flew from Los Angeles to Washington, D.C., in just over an hour.

6000 E Valencia Rd., Tucson, AZ 85706, 520-574-0462
Pimaair.org

TIP

The museum is massive, and you should plan on dedicating at least a day to explore. To begin, consider taking the fifty-minute guided Highlights of Aviation tour. Volunteer docents will give you the layout of the museum and point out some of the most significant displays in the main hangar. Feel free to ask them questions; they are quite knowledgeable and more than willing to share their expertise about the museum and its aircraft.

39

VISIT
THE THRIVING GHOST TOWN OF JEROME, ARIZONA

A living ghost town, Jerome sits atop Cleopatra Hill in Prescott National Forest. Take the scenic drive up the mountain to this tiny little city that is literally sliding down the mountainside. Once a thriving mining town that had miners pulling tons of gold, silver, and copper out of the earth and dumping millions of dollars into the local economy and the pockets of investors, that suddenly ceased when the ground began to rumble and shift—breaking windows, cracking foundations, and moving the town down the mountain inches at a time. After seventy-five years of mining, the tunneling simply proved too much and the town population dropped from thousands to double digits. Today, the entire town is considered a national historic landmark, and among the gutted buildings and languishing foundations are great restaurants, cozy bed and breakfasts, unique shops, and one-of-a-kind museums.

Jerome, AZ, azjerome.com

TIP

Make a weekend out of a visit to Jerome. Stay at the Jerome Grand Hotel (once the local hospital and asylum), reserve a room at a bed and breakfast, or head north down the mountain into Cottonwood or Clarkdale for a wine tasting and a stay at one of the local hotels. If you continue north, you'll find yourself headed directly into the red rock vistas of Sedona where you'll find resorts, inns, B&Bs, and plenty more to see and do.

40

TOUR
THE GHOSTLY HISTORY OF ARIZONA'S TERRITORIAL CAPITAL

Prescott was originally founded in 1864 as the capital of the territory of Arizona. This was long before Phoenix was settled and even before Tucson made its ten-year grab for the territorial seat of power. Prescott held its title until 1867, then regained it from 1877 until 1889 when Phoenix became the new capital of the Arizona Territory. Given its lengthy history as a frontier mining town in the Wild West, Prescott has had its share of notorious behavior—from gambling halls and underground speakeasies to brothels and opium dens. It's no surprise that ghost hunters have found the area rife with spirits and if you're up for a spooky tour of the Old West, this is one you won't want to miss. The tour, led by Darlene Wilson, not only touches on the ghost stories, but also hits some of the area's landmarks like the Hassayampa Inn and the Palace Saloon on Whiskey Row, and you'll also hear about some of the Old West legends who passed through Prescott.

928-642-5074, Ahauntingexperiencetours.com
Visit-prescott.com, darlene@ahauntingexperiencetours.com

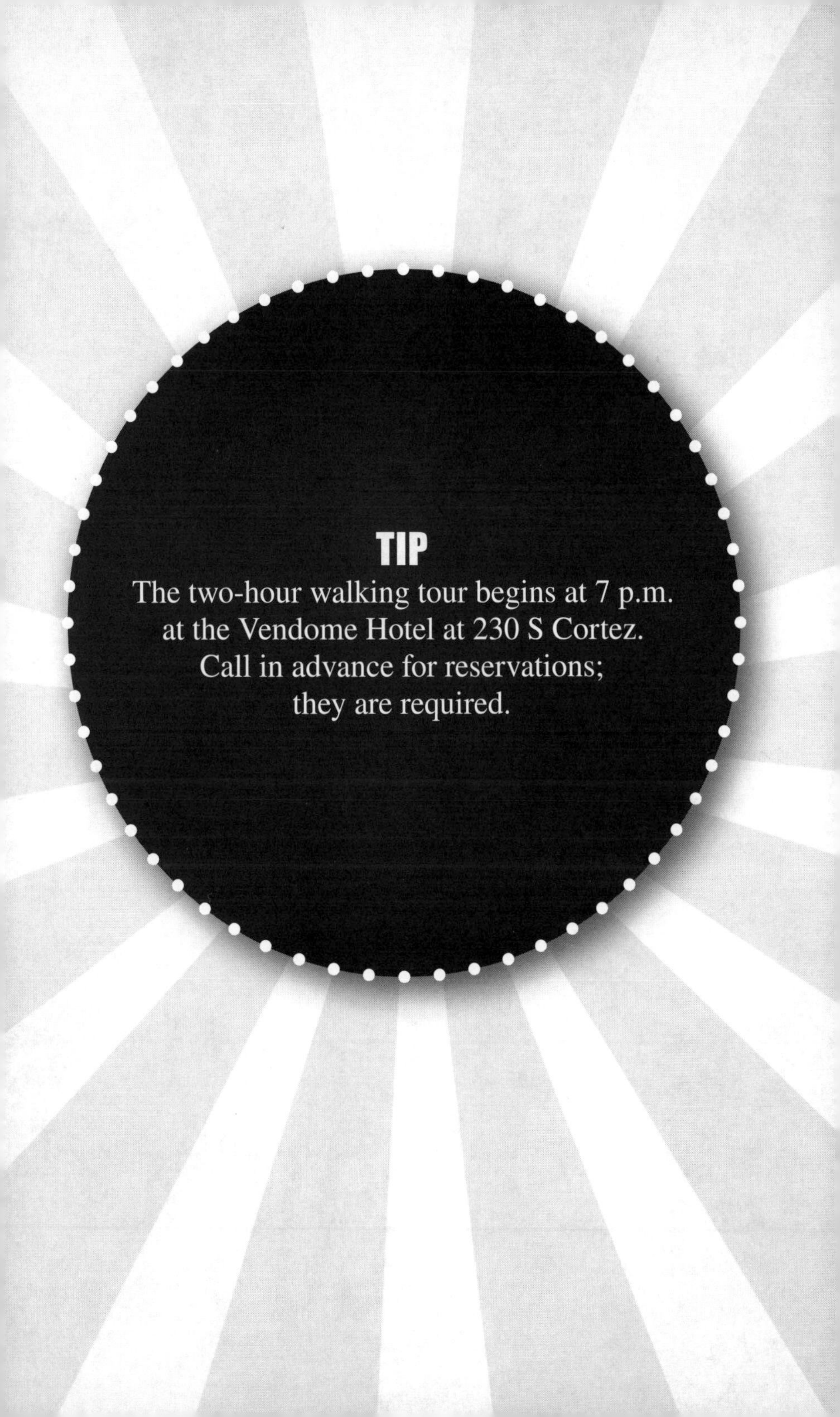

TIP

The two-hour walking tour begins at 7 p.m. at the Vendome Hotel at 230 S Cortez. Call in advance for reservations; they are required.

BUFFALO CHIP
SALOON

MUSIC AND ENTERTAINMENT

SAMPLE YOUR WAY
THROUGH THE ANNUAL CHOCOLATE AFFAIRE IN GLENDALE

While we can thank the likes of Richard Cadbury, Milton Hershey, and Russell Stover for popularizing the delightful marriage between chocolate and Valentine's Day, Glendale, home of the Cerreta Candy Company, does its part in perpetuating the tasty tradition. For more than twenty years, the city has hosted its annual Chocolate Affaire—usually in late January/ early February. Celebrating all things chocolate and everything romantic, the event hosts about forty chocolatiers at Murphy Park in historic downtown Glendale. Taste your way through this line-up of delectable chocolates and chocolate-covered treats, listen to live music, and witness what has become the largest annual gathering of romance writers in the Southwest. Local shops and restaurants in the area participate too, offering chocolate-themed drinks, treats, cookies, cakes, and even pancakes. Bring your sweet tooth, an empty stomach, and, of course, your heart.

Murphy Park, 58th and Glendale Avenues, Historic Downtown Glendale
www.glendaleaz.com/events/chocolateaffaire.cfm

BOOGIE THE NIGHT AWAY
AT THE RHYTHM ROOM

The Rhythm Room Roots, Blues & Concert Club hosts live music nightly to a crowded room and an even more crowded dance floor. Located in central Phoenix, this unassuming bar set back from Indian School Road showcases some of the hottest bands in the Valley and the U.S. playing Motown, soul, funk, and classic blues. You'll hear the likes of local favorite Soul Power, young up-and-comers like the Native American blues trio the Plateros from New Mexico, and blues legends like pianist Henry Gray. If you're here to listen, take a seat at the bar. If you plan to get up and move to the rhythm, grab a stool at the counter along the dance floor, or better yet, arrive early enough to snag one of the small tables up near the band.

1019 E Indian School Rd., Phoenix, AZ 85014, 602-265-4842
RhythmRoom.com

TIP

Doors open about an hour before showtime. Bring cash; there's a cover charge at the door. Arrive earlier for the best seats. You can chat while the band sets up.

EXPLORE
THE CULTURES OF THE WORLD WITH YOUR EARS AT MIM

The Musical Instrument Museum, affectionately known as MIM, is the only museum devoted entirely to music from across the globe. The interactive museum uses a combination of technology, live performances, workshops, and demonstrations to celebrate the music as well as the instruments, instrument making, musicians, songwriters, and craftsmen who bring music to life. Its collection includes more than fifteen thousand instruments and artifacts, and at least six thousand are on display at any given time, representing almost two hundred countries and territories. For that reason alone, you'll need more than a day to explore it. And you don't want to miss out on something exciting, like the hands-on Experience Gallery where you can play instruments from around the world, or the Artist Gallery showcasing the instruments of famous musicians like John Lennon and Carlos Santana, or Geographical Galleries, which present the music of Latin America or Southeast Asia or Africa. Also check out MIM's acoustically sound Music Theater, which hosts about two hundred live performances annually before an intimate crowd of three hundred. And the list goes on.

4725 E Mayo Blvd., Phoenix, AZ 85050, 480-478-6000
Mim.org

MIM can be a full-day experience; better yet, set aside time for a return trip. When you arrive, don a pair of wireless headphones, and as you move from exhibit to exhibit you'll hear the sounds of the music matching the display.

REVEL

IN AN INTIMATE MUSICAL PERFORMANCE AT TCA ART GALLERY

For an intimate musical experience, consider attending one of only a handful of annual performances of the Hayden Ferry Chamber Music Series produced by Catherine Hayden (of the Hayden Family that founded Tempe). The performances are held on Sundays at 2:30 p.m. from October through May at the Tempe Center for the Arts. The Gallery at TCA is a thirty-five-hundred-square-foot space dedicated to highlighting revolving bodies of work and makes for an ideal location for a small live musical performance. A beautiful blend of art and music, the airy space creates an intimate musical experience for locals and tourists alike where you can discover global musicians like the Paris-based Hermes Quartet performing Mozart and the U.S.-based baritone Michael Meraw accompanied by pianist Tanya Blalch performing music of the Civil War.

700 W Rio Salado Pkwy., Tempe, AZ 85281, 480-350-2829
Haydensferrychambermusicseries.org

45

LISTEN

TO LIVE MUSIC FRIDAY NIGHTS AT THE DESERT BOTANICAL GARDEN

Home to more than fifty thousand species of plants from deserts all over the world, the Desert Botanical Garden is a 145-acre desert oasis on the border of Phoenix and Tempe. The meandering paths lead visitors through a colorful exploration of vegetation from the purplish green pads of the prickly pear to the tiny yellow flowers of the foothill paloverde tree. Add a canopy of velvet black with pinpricks of light and live music wafting across the Ullman Terrace and it's truly a blend of the very best of what Phoenix has to offer. The garden hosts a spring Music in the Garden series from early February through late June featuring Latin jazz, the Phoenix Boys Choir, and other live performers from around the world. You'll also find a cash bar and appetizers.

1201 N Galvin Pkwy., Phoenix, AZ 85008, 480-941-1225
DBG.org—call 480-481-8188

CELEBRATE
THE SEASON WITH LIGHTS

To celebrate the holiday season, the Phoenix Zoo hosts Zoolights, an annual event with almost four million lights and seven hundred light displays spread out across the twenty-five acres of the zoo. This spectacular event is a sight to see and is one of the largest light displays in the Southwest. Also at Papago Park, the Desert Botanical Garden hosts their annual Las Noches de las Luminarias during the Christmas season. Each year for a little over two weeks, the garden comes alive with ice skating, holiday music, hot cocoa, and cider, and the paths are aglow with the light of more than eight thousand luminarias. On the west side of town Glendale hosts its annual Glendale Glitter, a holiday light display that includes 1.5 million lights decorating more than sixteen blocks of the city's historic downtown neighborhoods. The Glitter and Glow event in early January is the grand finale party, which concludes with live music, lots of lights, and about twenty giant, glowing hot air balloons.

455 N Galvin Pkwy., Phoenix, AZ 85008, 602-286-3800
Phoenixzoo.org

1201 N Galvin Pkwy, Phoenix, AZ 85008, 480-941-1225
Dbg.org

Murphy Park, 58th and Glendale Avenues, Historic Downtown Glendale
Glendaleaz.com

TIP

Zoolights is open nightly from 5:30 p.m. to 10:30 p.m., early November through early January; check their website for specific start/end dates and details about purchasing tickets. Check the DBG website beginning in late September for information about Las Noches de las Luminarias. And visit GlendaleAZ.com for details about this year's Glendale Glitters events.

GET YOUR GROOVE ON
AT TALKING STICK RESORT

Talking Stick Resort is among the Valley's newest resorts and casinos, and contains a full menu of entertainment options from slot machines and black jack tables on the casino floor to the Valley's highest nightclub, Degree 270, on the 14th floor. If dancing to DJs spinning the hottest tunes isn't your thing, try a mellower evening in the piano lounge just off the casino floor, or sip scotch and smoke a stogie at Shadows Lounge. There are several dinner options, but for the most spectacular view in Scottsdale try outdoor dining at Orange Sky on the 15th floor—overlooking Scottsdale and the Talking Stick Golf Course. For something milder, try the Patio outside on Friday and Saturday nights.

9800 E Indian Bend Rd., Scottsdale, AZ 85256, 480-850-7777
TalkingStickResort.com

LINE UP
FOR COUNTRY LINE DANCING LESSONS AT HANDLEBARJ IN SCOTTSDALE

HandlebarJ in Scottsdale is a forty-year-old landmark. Owned by the Herndon family and showcasing the Herndon Brothers band, Wednesdays through Sundays, you'll find a little taste of what Scottsdale was once like—cattle ranching cowboys and country western music. Stop in for line dancing lessons on Tuesday nights and brush up on your boot scootin' boogie before you head back out for dinner and dancing on Fridays and Saturdays. This is where you'll want to wear those cowboy boots and that cowboy hat you picked up at Bischoff's in Old Town Scottsdale earlier in the day. HandlebarJ also offers free dance lessons on Wednesdays so you can two-step your way around the floor like a pro. You'll find live music seven nights a week, but double-check their website in summer as sometimes hours vary.

7116 E Becker Ln., Scottsdale, AZ 85254, 480-948-0110
HandlebarJ.com

RIDE THE LIGHT RAIL
FOR A NIGHT ON THE TOWN

Depending on where you're staying in the Valley, you can hop on the Valley Metro Light Rail and ride it from the west side of town at 19th Avenue and Montebello to Sycamore and Main in Mesa. The light rail passes directly through ASU's Tempe campus, putting you a short walk from all of the entertainment and dining in downtown Tempe. It also passes through downtown Phoenix, including the thriving artists' district of Roosevelt Row. The light rail, completed in 2008, runs seven days a week and almost twenty-four hours on weekends. If you're headed to downtown Tempe, get off at the Mill Avenue/Third Street station; if you're looking for the restaurants and nightlife of Roosevelt Row get off at the Roosevelt/Central Avenue station. Purchase an all-day pass at the ticket kiosks for unlimited jumps on and off the rail as you make your way to and from your destination.

Valleymetro.org, DowntownTempe.com, RooseveltRow.org

50

PARTAKE IN BOOKS AND BREW

AT CHANGING HANDS IN CENTRAL PHOENIX

Changing Hands, a local Tempe bookstore and community stronghold for more than forty years, decided to capitalize on the success of its Tempe location by creating an innovative concept that blends three essential community elements (pub, coffee shop, and bookstore). In doing so, they created one spectacular "third place"—the First Draft Book Bar. Located at the northern end of Phoenix's thriving uptown area, the double entendre (first draft) encompasses two of its major attractions (books and beer). You'll also find coffee, pub snacks, and wine, and in the spirit of its indie bookstore roots, First Draft showcases only local food vendors. Stop in for a beer, a coffee, or to simply browse the books. The store also hosts community events like ping-pong tournaments and game nights.

300 W Camelback Rd., Phoenix, 602-274-0067
changinghands.com/firstdraftbar

ROCK OUT
TO OUTLAW COUNTRY MUSIC AT THE RUSTY SPUR

One of the smallest bars you'll find in the Valley, it's also one of the most packed and popular. Located in Old Town Scottsdale, the Rusty Spur Saloon, once the site of the Farmers' Bank of Scottsdale, recently celebrated its sixtieth year as Scottsdale's first saloon. This postage stamp–sized bar attracts country music fans from all walks of life. On any given night you'll find yuppies, millennials, retirees, bikers, and even a few college students dancing together on the tiny dance floor. The Rusty Spur hosts live music most afternoons and evenings, but Thursdays through Saturdays from 8 p.m. until after midnight you'll hear the siren call of the very rowdy Psychobilly Rodeo Band drawing you in off the streets belting out country and southern rock classics by Johnny Cash, Waylon Jennings, George Strait, and Lynyrd Skynyrd.

7245 E Main St., Scottsdale, AZ 85251, 480-425-7787
rustyspursaloon.com

TIP

If you're looking to sit at one of the few tables on Friday or Saturday night, arrive a little before the band starts at 8 p.m. If you get there later, expect to get cozy with your neighbors in what will quickly become standing room only. Everyone is fun and friendly—don't be afraid to squeeze in and claim your spot, because no matter how late you get there they'll make a path for you to get to the bar to grab your drink.

52

SIP A CAPPUCCINO
AT JAZZ NIGHT AT GOLD BAR IN TEMPE

Tempe is the original home of Arizona State University. Perhaps these college town roots were the catalyst for the numerous independent coffee shops that dot the area and continue to sprout up in and around Tempe's neighborhoods. These local favorites have loyal followers for various reasons—like the on-site roasting beans at Cartel Coffee Lab, the French-press-only brew at Steve's Espresso, and the welcoming feel of Gold Bar Espresso where it seems that everyone does know your name. Located on the northeast corner of McClintock and Southern, the family-owned Gold Bar is where coffee lovers can sit outside on Friday and Sunday evenings sipping lattes and listening to live jazz. Saturdays are game nights, and as Karen (who owns Gold Bar with her husband, Dennis) says, "bring the whole family."

TIP

Stop by Cartel Coffee Lab in the evenings where you can get two kinds of brew—coffee and their coffee-inspired beer.

225 W University Dr., #101, Tempe, AZ, 480-225-3899
7124 E 5th Ave., Scottsdale, AZ, 480-269-3172
Cartelcoffeelab.com

3141 S McClintock Dr., Tempe, AZ 85282, 480-839-3082
Goldbarespresso.org

1801 E Baseline Rd., #102, Tempe, AZ 85283, 480-777-5373
Stevesespresso.com

AMBLE DOWN THE FAIRWAY

AT THE ARIZONA STATE FAIR

The sights, the smells, and the sounds of the Arizona State Fair will transport you from the urban landscape surrounding the Arizona State Fairgrounds in central Phoenix to the middle of some cattle ranch on the outskirts of town. It may even take you back a few decades to a point in time when eating a deep-fried Twinkie seemed like a great idea because the consequences of those calories never even crossed your mind. The Arizona State Fair is a tradition older than the state itself. The first fair, held in the fall of 1884, was actually a territorial fair since Arizona wouldn't become a state until 1912. Held in the fall—usually mid-October into early November—the Arizona State Fair showcases top entertainers, death-defying thrill rides, spectacular attractions, and a lot of batter-dipped food you won't find anywhere else.

1826 W McDowell Rd., Phoenix, AZ 85007, 602-252-6771
Azstatefair.com

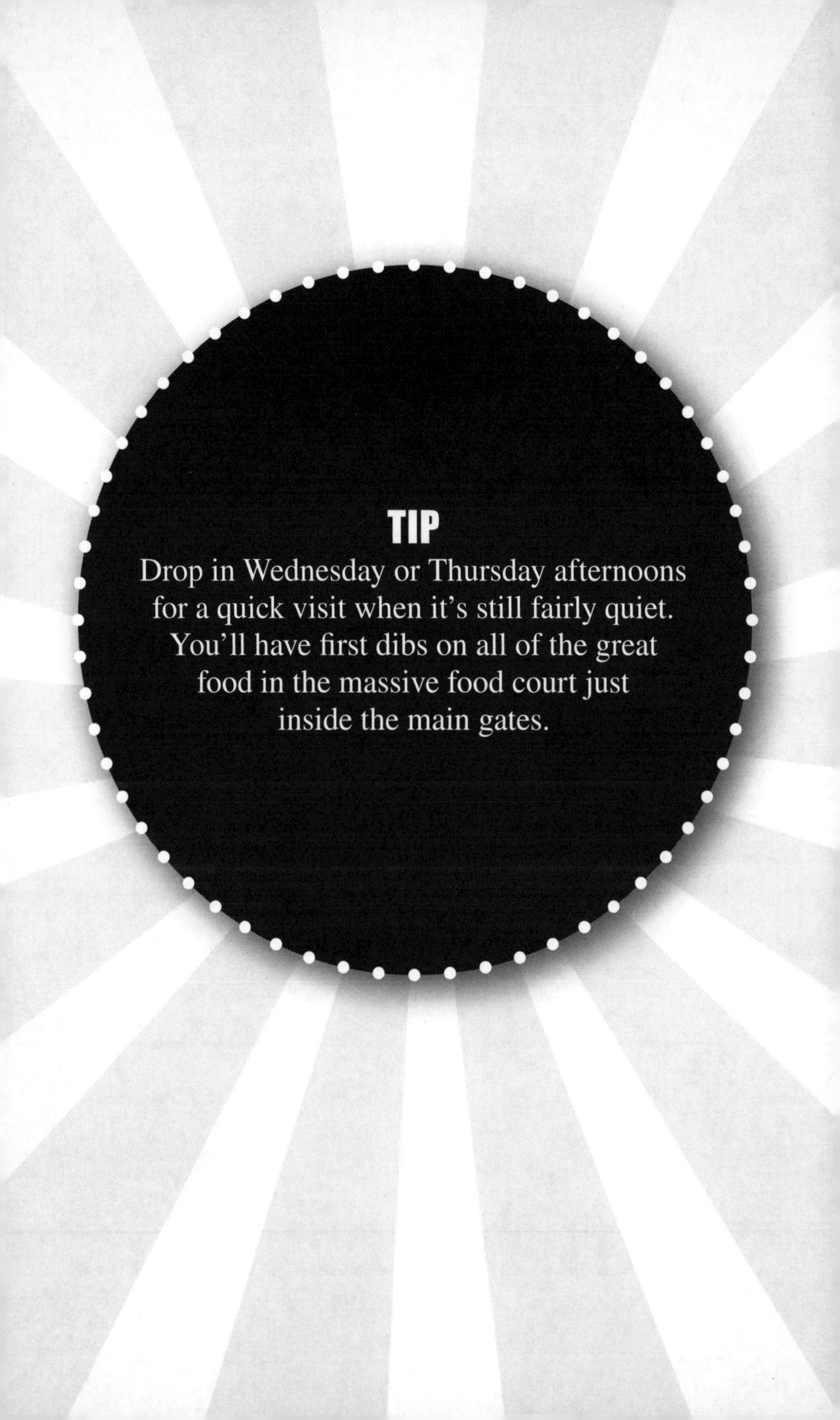

TIP

Drop in Wednesday or Thursday afternoons for a quick visit when it's still fairly quiet. You'll have first dibs on all of the great food in the massive food court just inside the main gates.

GAMBLE
AT THE CASINOS

The state of Arizona is home to twenty-one Native American tribes, and the Phoenix metropolitan area includes four communities: the Ak-Chin Indian and Gila River Indian Communities to the south, the Salt River Pima-Maricopa Indian Community to the east, and the Fort McDowell Yavapai Nation to the northeast. Between them they have built eight casinos in and around Phoenix. Depending on where you go, you'll find slot machines, blackjack and poker tables, Vegas-worthy buffets, headline performers, championship golf courses, and premier spas. Several of the casinos have been coupled with some of the area's best resorts, including Talking Stick Resort in Scottsdale and Wild Horse Pass Hotel & Casino in Chandler. Both resorts offer a mix of gaming, spa, golf, desert views, and spectacular dining.

Casino Arizona (Scottsdale)
524 N 92nd St., Scottsdale, AZ 85256
480-850-7777

Cliff Castle Casino Hotel (Camp Verde)
555 W Middle Verde Rd., Camp Verde, AZ, 86322
928-567-7999

Fort McDowell Casino (Scottsdale)
10424 N Fort McDowell Rd., Fort McDowell, AZ 85264
800-843-3678

Harrah's Ak-Chin Casino (Maricopa)
15406 N Maricopa Rd, Maricopa, AZ 85139
480-802-5000

Lone Butte Casino (Chandler)
1077 S Kyrene Rd, Chandler, AZ 85226
520-796-7777

Talking Stick Resort (Scottsdale)
800 E Indian Bend Rd, Scottsdale, AZ 85256
480-850-7777

Vee Quiva Hotel & Casino (Laveen)
15091 Komatke Ln, Laveen Village, AZ 85339
800-946-4452

Wild Horse Pass Hotel & Casino (Chandler)
5040 Wild Horse Pass Blvd, Chandler, AZ 85226
800-946-4452

55

NIGHT AT THE IMPROV
IN TEMPE

The Tempe Improv has a long history of hosting some of the best stand-up comics in the country. While the historic comedy club closed for about a year, it reopened again in 2013 to once again host comedic headliners such as Jamie Kennedy, Frank Caliendo, Adam Ferrera, and Pauly Shore. Located just east of ASU's Tempe campus, the recently renovated space sits alongside local music and grub pub Copper Blues. Pair a funny evening with great music by local favorites like Lee Perreira and the Ryan Sims Band. The floor-to-ceiling glass doors at Copper Blue are open most of the year, offering a warm breeze and great views of Tempe at night.

930 E University Dr., Tempe, AZ 85281, 480-921-9877
Tempeimprov.com

930 E University Dr., #208, Tempe, AZ 85281, 480-376-1243
Copperblueslive.com

WITHSTAND THE FORCES OF NATURE

AT THE ARIZONA SCIENCE CENTER

The Arizona Science Center, located at Heritage and Science Park in the heart of downtown Phoenix, creates an experiential opportunity for visitors of all ages to play and learn about the world around us. The center has harnessed the forces of nature in a permanent exhibit designed to give you both an adrenaline rush and a greater respect for Mother Nature. Long enough to get your blood pumping and safe enough that you'll walk away unscathed, the exhibit's Immersion Theater gives guests a five-minute glimpse at what it might be like in the middle of a forest fire, tornado, hurricane, monsoon, and volcanic eruption. Once you've survived the forces of nature, you can wander into any of the other exciting, though less heart-stopping, exhibits.

600 E Washington St., Phoenix, AZ 85004, 602-716-2000
Azscience.org

SLIP AND SLIDE
YOUR WAY THROUGH THE SUMMER HEAT

Arizona temperatures may soar in the summer, but the resort prices dip considerably, making the summertime an ideal time to cool off at some of the area's resorts. Many of them, like the Wigwam Resort in Litchfield Park in the West Valley, Arizona Grand Resort's Oasis Water Park in south Phoenix, and Pointe Hilton Squaw Peak Resort in north Phoenix, feature fun in the sun with steep, water-soaked slides, waterfalls, and kid-friendly pools. You'll also find golf courses, on-property dining, events and activities, and even spas—making it a family vacation everyone will love. Check out the recently renovated Hyatt Regency Scottsdale Resort & Spa at Gainey Ranch, where you'll find a 2.5-acre water playground that even adults will enjoy in the summer heat.

7677 N 16th St., Phoenix, AZ 85020, 602-997-2626
Squawpeakhilton.com

8000 Arizona Grand Pkwy., Phoenix, AZ 85044, 602-438-9000
Arizonagrandresort.com

300 E Wigwam Blvd., Litchfield Park, AZ 85340, 623-935-3811
Wigwamarizona.com

7500 E Doubletree Ranch Rd, Scottsdale, AZ 85258, 480-444-1234
Scottsdale.hyatt.com

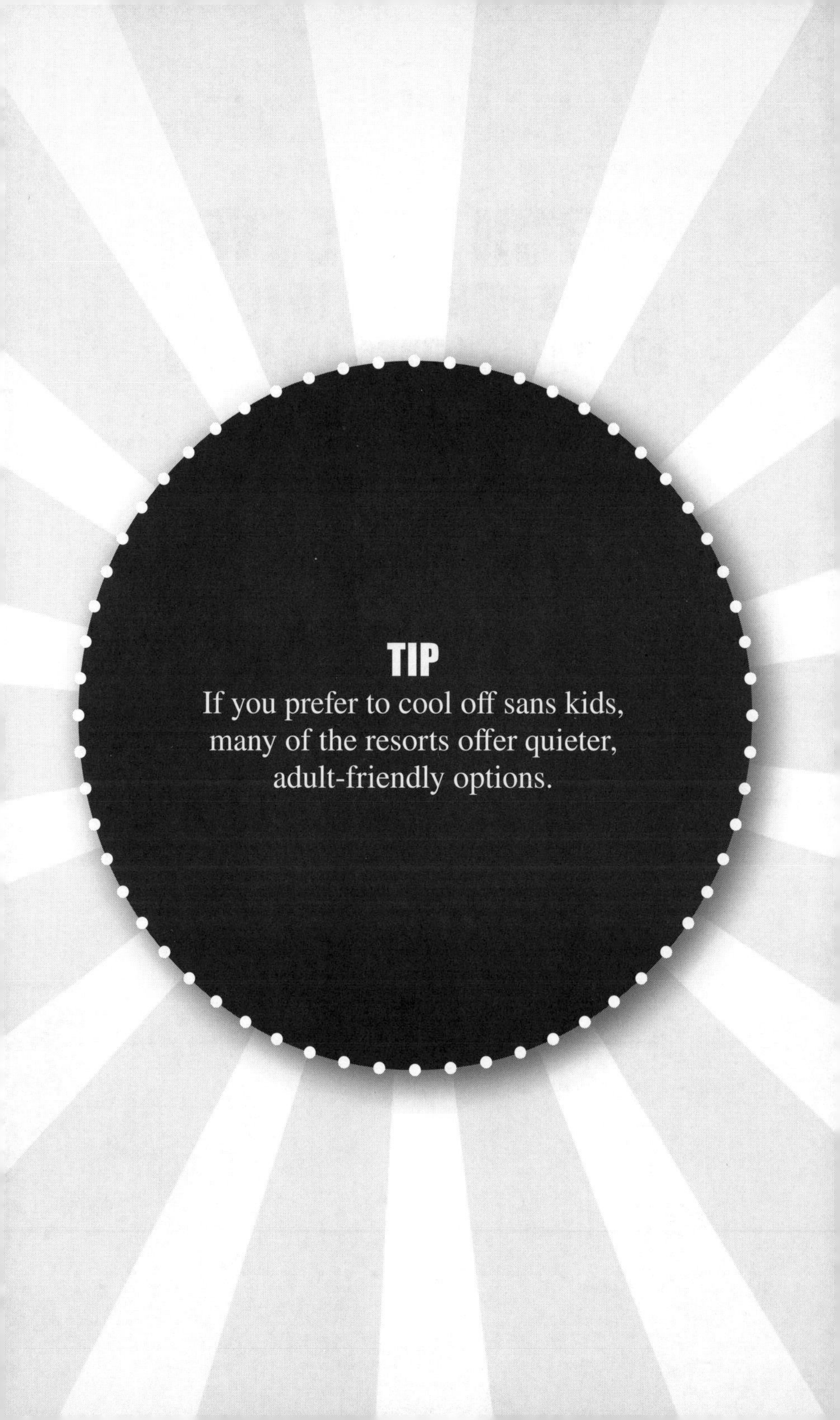
TIP
If you prefer to cool off sans kids,
many of the resorts offer quieter,
adult-friendly options.

WATCH WIDE-EYED
AS THE FIGHTER JETS FLY BY AT THE LUKE DAYS AIR SHOW

Luke Air Force Base in Glendale is the training base for many of the air force's most elite fighter pilots, and since 1941 has trained more than sixty thousand aviators. Named for the very first pilot to receive the Medal of Honor—World War I fighter pilot and Arizona native son Second Lieutenant Frank Luke Jr.—Luke Air Force Base's 56th Fighter Wing hosts Luke Days Air Show each March. Free and open to the public, this annual event brings out about 150,000 visitors each day. The two-day event features both aerial performances by airmen as well as aircraft displays. The air force base recently began training airmen on the F-35 Lightning II, which is displayed along with the famous F-16 Fighting Falcon.

14185 Falcon St., Glendale, AZ 85309, 623-856-5853
Luke.af.mil

CLIMB ROCK WALLS
AT PHOENIX ROCK GYM

The towering cliffs and scalable rock faces across the surrounding landscape may very well inspire you to start rock climbing. Test your skills at the Phoenix Rock Gym before you head out into the wild Sonoran Desert. Located in Tempe near the ASU campus, this rock gym offers more than fifteen thousand square feet of ever-changing climbing surfaces. The gym is open to both novices and hard-core rock climbers honing their skills, and offers all types of surfaces requiring all levels of skills, including a bouldering area that might just come in handy if you're thinking of climbing around any of our giant granite boulders. You'll get a video and hands-on orientation from a PRG staffer on your first visit, but after that you can tie in on the next available rope and start climbing.

1353 E University Dr,, Tempe, AZ 85281, 480-921-8322
Phoenix Rock Gym

TIP

You can bring your own gear or rent from the gym.

60

SURF THE BIG WAVES
IN THE DESERT

Built in 1969, Big Surf Water Park in Tempe is the country's oldest waterpark. Its second claim to fame is the third-largest wave pool in the world. In addition to the 2.5 million gallon Waikiki Beach Wave Pool, the park has towering slides that twist and turn their way into cool pools of clear water for the daredevils in the family, and for little ones just starting out there are the wading pools and mini-slides. The park's newest attraction is the zip line that races three hundred feet from one end of the Waikiki Beach to the other. Weekends are a zoo, but consider a weekday visit in summer to cool off at one cool place.

500 N McClintock Dr., Tempe, AZ 85281, 480-994-2297
BigSurfFun.com, castlesncoasters.com, golfland.com/Mesa

For more water fun try Golfland Sun Splash in Mesa at 155 West Hampton Ave. or for roller coaster rides try Castles 'N Coasters in Phoenix off I-17 at 9445 North Metro Parkway East.

CULTURE AND HISTORY

ENCOUNTER
ARIZONA'S NATIVE AMERICAN CULTURES WITH NATIVE TRAILS

Sponsored by the Fort McDowell Yavapai Nation, Native Trails celebrates the cultural heritage of the first North American inhabitants. The one-hour event, held every Thursday and Saturday from January through April at Scottsdale Civic Park, highlights the art, music, and native dances of the Hopi, Dine (Navajo), Akimel Au-Auth, and San Carlos Apache tribes of Arizona. It's a beautiful time of year to spread blankets on the lawn and listen to the thumping drums, high-pitched flutes, and chanting as men and women perform the traditions and customs of their native tribes. Guests may even find themselves dancing to the contagious beat of the round dance—a friendship and courting dance designed to engage participation. The event takes place from noon to 1 p.m.

7375 E 2nd St., Scottsdale, AZ 85251
www.experiencescottsdale.com/event/native-trails

TIP

Year-round you can also find Native American dances performed by Arizona tribespeople at the Fountain Court at the Hyatt Regency Scottsdale Resort off Via de Ventura in north Scottsdale.

62

WITNESS
THE WORLD CHAMPIONSHIP HOOP DANCE CONTEST

Each February for two days the lawns of the Heard Museum on Central Avenue in downtown Phoenix fill with spectators who gather to watch dancers from the U.S. and Canada compete for top spot as the world champion hoop dancer. The Hoop Dance or "dance of life" is a beautiful example of custom, athleticism, speed, creativity, showmanship, and rhythm as both men and women incorporate a unique blend of cultural tradition and personal style to weave an intricate story that they tell with the hoops. The dance may use only a few hoops or more than fifty as dancers capture the audience's attention with intricate designs, choreography, and movement to represent the animals, symbols, and story elements.

2301 N Central Ave., Phoenix, AZ 85004, 602-252-8840
Heard.org/event/hoop

ENJOY AN OUTDOOR EVENING PERFORMANCE OF BALLET UNDER THE STARS

Take the beautiful, graceful Arizona Ballet, add the delightful fall weather of Phoenix, and put it all on stage at the Tempe Center for the Arts outdoor amphitheater for a performance unlike any you'll ever find—Ballet under the Stars. The Arizona Ballet hosts five of these breathtaking performances each year in late September through early October at select locations around the Valley. Each location is an ideal outdoor setting; complete with lighting, costumes, and music, it's truly an Arizona experience. Despite the significant expense of presenting such events, performances are free and open to the public. Bring your blankets or lawn chairs and find a spot to take it all in. Performances range from the classical to the contemporary.

TIP

Check the Arizona Ballet website for performances all across the Valley.
balletaz.org/community-outreach/ballet-under-the-stars

Beardsley Park, Sun City West
12755 Beardsley Rd., Sun City West, AZ
623-544-6524

Estrella Lakeside Amphitheater, Goodyear
10300 S Estrella Pkwy., Goodyear, AZ 85338
623-386-1000

Steele Indian School Park, Phoenix
300 E Indian School Rd. (3rd St. and Indian School Rd.)
Phoenix, AZ 85012
602-534-4810

Tempe Center for the Arts Amphitheater, Tempe
700 W Rio Salado Pkwy, Tempe, AZ 85281
480-350-2829

Fountain Park, Fountain Hills
13029 N Saguaro Blvd., Fountain Hills, AZ 85268
480-816-5100

CHECK OUT THE COWBOY ART
AT THE PHOENIX ART MUSEUM

In the spirit of Arizona's Wild West heritage, the Phoenix Art Museum houses a Western American collection highlighting art and artists of the American Southwest from the nineteenth and twentieth centuries. Their work captures the wide open spaces of the Western plains, rugged cowboy culture, and Native American themes and subjects. The collection includes Georgia O'Keeffe's large-scale depictions of northern New Mexico; the oil paintings and bronze sculptures of cowboys, soldiers, and Native Americans of the Old West by Frederic Remington; pieces like the beautiful bronze sculpture *Sun Vow* by Hermon Atkins MacNeil; and local scenes like the oil painting *Chain of Spires along the Gila River* by John Mix Stanley.

1625 N Central Ave., Phoenix, AZ 85004, 602-257-1222
www.phxart.org

TIP

Also at the Phoenix Art Museum is Claude Monet's *Les Arceaux Fleuris, Giverny*. You'll also find Yayoi Kusama's *Swarm of Fireflies*; check out this very cool experience in the Contemporary Art Collection.

65

LISTEN
TO THE PHOENIX SYMPHONY BRING MUSIC TO LIFE

Passionately dedicated to bringing music to life for music lovers of all ages and musical tastes, the Phoenix Symphony has introduced a series of musical performances that span the traditional to the contemporary. Introducing a multimedia experience of sight and sound, the symphony has brought forth inspiring and moving performances like the Tribute to the Brave, which celebrates the lives of those who fought for our freedom and brings to light the music and the memories of the time. In addition to the beautiful, traditional, symphonic compositions of Mozart, Beethoven, Brahms, and Ravel, the Phoenix Symphony has also introduced contemporary music from composers like John Williams, who has written the music for such aurally iconic movies as *E.T.*, *Harry Potter*, *Indiana Jones*, *Jaws,* and *Star Wars*.

75 N 2nd St., Phoenix, AZ 85004, 602-262-6225
Phoenixsymphony.org

TIP
Check out the Phoenix Symphony's concert and event schedule online at phoenixsymphony.org. Note performance locations as the symphony performs around the Valley.

MEET
THE ARTIST IN RESIDENCE AT LON'S AT THE HERMOSA

In keeping with the spirit of its original owner and cowboy artist Lon Magargee, LON's continues its artist-in-residence series. Showcasing the work and expertise of creatives like contemporary artist Mike Elsass, mixed-medium artist and Arizona native Gina Richmann, fashion icon Robert Black, and award-winning author Karen MacNeil, LON's hosts an interactive event with the artist, including brunch or dinner, and a talk or presentation given by the artist. The food is delicious and the artists inspiring.

5532 N Palo Cristi Rd., Paradise Valley, AZ 85253, 602-955-7878
Hermosainn.com

ARTWALK THE LINE
THROUGH SCOTTSDALE'S ARTS DISTRICT

Just about every Thursday for the last forty years, the sidewalks along Main Street and Marshall Way in downtown Scottsdale have filled with strolling couples, sidewalk musicians, and groups of gallery goers looking for an excuse, any excuse really, to delight in the beautiful art that fills the shops, galleries, and boutiques in the Marshall Way Arts District. The Scottsdale ArtWalk, hosted by the Scottsdale Gallery Association, helps bring art to life for locals and tourists alike. No matter the heat, the ArtWalk is held from 7 p.m. to 9 p.m. every Thursday (except Thanksgiving). The arts district galleries and studios feature a wide spectrum of art and artists from the contemporary to cowboy art and include painters, artisans, jewelry makers, pottery makers, and sculptors.

480-998-4323, scottsdalegalleries.com

TIP

Have a favorite artisan? Many of the galleries use Thursdays as their open-house night for featured artists. Check the gallery's website for details. Not here on a Thursday night? Visit the association's website for a map of the galleries in the area and visit during regular business hours. On the sidewalks you'll find "ArtWalk the Line" logos pointing the way.

TAKE
THE FREE LOCAL MOTION TROLLEY TOUR OF DOWNTOWN SCOTTSDALE

A blend of rugged charm and elegant sophistication, Scottsdale is a mecca for artists and art both old and new. Local art and architecture expert Ace Bailey created Ultimate Art & Cultural Tours to prominently feature the beautiful art and artistry of the Southwest and the talented artists who create it. One of her most popular tours is the Local Motion Downtown Tour—a great way to see downtown Scottsdale. Every second Saturday of the month, you can pick up this tour at 10 a.m. at the Old Adobe Mission at 1st and Brown. The two-hour tour begins with the history of the mission and continues via trolley with a guided tour of the arts district, the iconic Hotel Valley Ho, and the SouthBridge and Waterfront shopping and dining districts.

Scottsdale, AZ 85251, 480-634-6850
Utlimatearttours.com

TIP

Seats are limited on the trolley, so be sure to make a reservation; you can do so by calling 480-634-6850. Ace also offers a one-of-a-kind gallery tour where she works with gallery owners and/or artists to provide a private showing and Q&A session about the gallery and the art. She also provides a Behind the Scenes Artist Studio Tour, which gives tour-goers an opportunity to meet the artist, see them work, and hear firsthand about their craft.

TOUR TOVREA CASTLE
AT CARRARO HEIGHTS

Some refer to it as the Castle, others as the Wedding Cake you can see from the Loop 202. When it was originally built by Italian immigrant Alessio Carraro in 1930, it was meant to be his crowning achievement and the hotel for his resort property. However, no one knows if it was the Great Depression or something else entirely that caused him to sell it just one year later to local meat-packer magnate E.A Tovrea and his wife, Della. Today, the Castle with its extensive desert gardens is considered a Phoenix Point of Pride and is open for docent-led tours most Fridays through Sundays, from January through June and again from September through December.

5025 E Van Buren St., Phoenix, AZ 85008, 602-256-3221
Tovreacastletours.com

TIP

Check the website for specific hours as they vary depending on the time of year.

FIRST FRIDAY
IN ROOSEVELT ROW DISTRICT

Since 1994, Artlink has hosted First Fridays in downtown Phoenix. Over the last two decades, the event has expanded to include more than one hundred galleries, studios, and art-related spaces and attracts between fourteen and twenty thousand patrons every first Friday of the month. The self-guided walking tour starts with a shuttle bus at Phoenix Art Museum that can drop you off at various stops along the way. There are countless restaurants, bars, and coffeehouses, as well as street vendors and live musicians across the downtown area. Stretching from Jefferson Street to McDowell Road and from 7th Street to just past 15th Avenue, Artlink First Fridays is considered the largest, self-guided art walk. Grab a First Friday Trolley Tour Map (you can also get it online) to find out what you want to see and where you want to go. The trolleys run from 6 p.m. to 10 p.m.

132 S Central Ave, Phoenix, AZ 85004, 602-256-7539
Artlinkphoenix.com

ATTEND THE ANNUAL
GREATER PHOENIX JEWISH FILM FESTIVAL

For a look at moving and entertaining films, check out this decades-old film festival, featuring Jewish-themed films from filmmakers around the world. Movies are carefully selected from a variety of genres including comedy, drama, documentary, and Holocaust films. Speakers and presentations accompany many of the films and include both Jewish and non-Jewish filmmakers, historians, and film critics. Held in February each year, films are shown across the Valley in venues in Chandler, Peoria, and Scottsdale and bring in more than five thousand viewers. The event is sponsored by local businesses and business owners across the Valley.

602-753-9366
Gpjff.org

TIP

Check the website for this year's schedule and film locations.

CATCH A GLIMPSE OF
TALIESIN'S FIRE-BREATHING DRAGON

For architecture enthusiasts, a trip to Taliesin West may be a trip to the Southwestern mecca of architecture. The architectural achievement of world-renowned architect Frank Lloyd Wright, Taliesin West is now a national historic landmark, but it was once Wright's home and school. Built in 1937, the estate stretches out over 620 acres in the McDowell Mountains. Strategically placed high above the desert floor and integrated into the desert landscape, it's a stunning intermingling of nature and architecture. For a truly unique look at this desert gem, take the Night Lights Tour. The two-hour tour leaves at 6:30 p.m., 7:00 p.m., and 7:15 p.m. on Fridays, and reveals some of the hidden secrets of Taliesin West that only come alive at night—like the warm glow of the home against the mountain backdrop and Wright's fire-breathing dragon.

12621 N Frank Lloyd Wright Blvd., Scottsdale, AZ 85259, 480-627-5340
Franklloydwright.org/Taliesin-west

TIP

Reservations are required; children age 13 and up are welcome for this evening tour.

73

DISCOVER
PHOENIX'S HISTORIC DISTRICTS

Established in 1881, the lineage of Phoenix's neighborhoods only stretches back to the turn of the twentieth century, but the city's residents have done their best (especially in recent decades) to preserve the architectural history of the city's neighborhoods. Annually and biannually, the residents of the historic Willo District and Encanto Park neighborhoods, respectively, open their homes, inviting visitors to appreciate the hard work it took to lovingly restore them to their original splendor. These events often turn into neighborhood-wide street fairs complete with entertainers, local artisans, live music, and delicious food as people wander down tree-lined streets from one home tour to the next. The Willo Home Tour is in early February each year and the Encanto-Palmcroft Tour runs every two years in March of odd years.

WilloDistrict.com, Encantopalmcroft.org

TIP

If you aren't able to make the tours, a drive through these beautiful neighborhoods will give you a glimpse of Phoenix at the turn of the century. For a map of each of the historic districts in Phoenix, visit historicphoenix.com and click on the historic districts link. Visit each tour's website for contact information for this year's volunteers.

TOUR PHOENIX AT THE TURN OF THE NINETEENTH CENTURY

The Rosson House, built in 1895, is the centerpiece of Heritage Square and Science Park, bordered on the north and south by Monroe and Washington Streets and on the east and west by 5th and 7th Streets in downtown Phoenix. Located within walking distance of several downtown landmarks including the Phoenix Convention Center, Arizona Science Center, and St. Mary's Basilica, the Rosson House has preserved what life was like for downtown Phoenix families in what was then the territorial capital of Arizona. Take a docent-led tour for a look at the Victorian architecture and living spaces of a pioneering family. Also in Heritage Square and Science Park are the historic Teeter House and Carriage House, Silva House, and the Baird Machine Shop, each of which has been converted into an eating establishment.

113 N 6th St., Phoenix, AZ 85004, 602-261-8063
RossonHouse.com

TIP

These sixty-minute tours are given Wednesdays through Sundays. You can order tickets online. Before or after the tour consider checking out one of the other landmarks by stopping by these restaurants: Nobuo at Teeter House, Pizzeria Bianco at the Baird Machine Shop, the Rose and Crown at the Silva House, and the Royal Coffee Bar at the Teeter Carriage House.

75

HAIL THE HEROES
AT THE HALL OF FLAME MUSEUM OF FIREFIGHTING

What began with a single 1924 fire engine in 1956 has turned into a tribute to firefighting and firefighters. Spanning the history of centuries of firefighting, the Hall of Flame Museum of Firefighting at Papago Park near the Phoenix Zoo and the Desert Botanical Garden displays the tools of the firefighting trade, and honors the fallen heroes who died in the line of duty, including a special memorial to the New York City firefighters, police, and Port Authority officers who died on September 11, 2001. Additionally, the museum shows how fires are fought, with a special exhibit for wildfires, and displays almost one hundred restored pieces dating back as far as the early part of the eighteenth century, including horse drawn-wagons and pumps from around the world.

6101 E Van Buren St., Phoenix, AZ 85008, 602-275-3473
Hallofflame.org

CLIMB TO THE LOWER CLIFF DWELLINGS
AT TONTO NATIONAL PARK

Located in the cliffs high above Roosevelt Lake and built by a group of prehistoric people that archaeologists have named the Salado, these ancient dwellings are still a sight to see. The seven-hundred-year-old lower cliff dwellings are set back against a cave-like space in the cliffs in the Tonto Basin and feature twenty separate rooms used for sleeping, eating, and cooking. The Salado used resources from the surrounding desert, including pine and juniper wood, to create their home and lived off the desert flora and fauna. Today, you can walk the short, but steep paved path to see the dwellings first hand. While the walls and rooms continue to crumble in the elements, you can catch a glimpse of the space where some of Arizona's earliest inhabitants once lived. Turn around and you'll also get an unprecedented look at the rich desert landscape of the Tonto Basin.

Tonto National Monument, 26260 N. AZ Hwy 188, Roosevelt AZ 85545
Nps.gov/tont

TIP

The gift shop in the park offers an array of books about Arizona and the park.

START AT THE LITTLE RED SCHOOLHOUSE

This sixty-minute, self-guided walking tour begins at the Little Red Schoolhouse at the edge of Civic Park Plaza off Main Street and ends at the Scottsdale Public Library, also on the Civic Park Plaza but across Drinkwater Boulevard. The little tour has fifteen fun-filled stops that share with you some of the highlights and historical landmarks of Old Town Scottsdale, including the Farmers State Bank of Scottsdale on the south side of Main (now the Rusty Spur Saloon). You'll also stop at Cavalliere's Blacksmith Shop. The adobe structure was built in 1920 and was once considered to be at the "edge of town." Another stop is the old olive trees lining Second Street, the remnants of a drought in the 1890s.

The Little Red Schoolhouse
7333 East Scottsdale Mall, Scottsdale, AZ 85251
www.experiencescottsdale.com/wp-content/uploads/2012/06/HistoricWalkingTourMap.pdf

TIP

Download and print the PDF, which gives you a map and a description of all the stops along the way. Or you can find one of the stops and take a photo of the painted map on the sidewalk to guide the way.

STRAY OFF THE BEATEN PATH
WITH STRAY CAT THEATRE

Stray Cat Theatre is independent dramatic art at its finest—quirky, thought-provoking, irreverent, and constantly pushing the theatrical envelope. With more than a decade under its belt, Stray Cat continues to afford local playwrights, actors, and artists a live forum for their art. The productions, of which there are typically only about four a season, may very well be works of satirical genius and can provoke shocked gasps as quickly and as often as unabashed laughter. For an entertaining evening out, consider one of their live performances at Tempe Center for the Arts, close to downtown Tempe's restaurant and bar scene, where you can grab dinner and a drink before or after the show.

480-227-1766, Straycattheatre.org

TIP

While Tempe Center for the Arts is their home base, Stray Cat's productions can travel. Check the website for show dates and locations.

79

WANDER THROUGH TIME
AT THE ARIZONA MUSEUM OF NATURAL HISTORY

Take an interactive trip through Arizona's history from its early days beneath the Paleozoic seas to a time when dinosaurs roamed the area. (Kids can dig for fossils in the Paleo Dig Pit outside.) Fast forward to the forefathers of the Native American tribes of today—the Hohokam, Anasazi, and Mogollon cultures—and the pueblo dwellings, trails, and canals they built. In more recent history, the museum, located in downtown Mesa, covers the Spanish explorers and provides an interactive look at the territorial days of Arizona as the state's five economic strongholds emerged—citrus, cattle, copper, cotton, and climate. Wander through a copper mine, get locked up in the territorial jail, and discover Arizona's role in the movie industry.

3 N Macdonald, Mesa, AZ 85201, 480-644-2230
Azmnh.org

80

TAKE THE MAGICAL HISTORY TOUR
OF THE HOTEL VALLEY HO

One of Ultimate Art & Cultural Tours's most popular tours, this tour covers both the original 1950s-style design of the iconic Hotel Valley Ho as well as the new elements incorporated when it was renovated at the turn of the twenty-first century. Built in 1956, Hotel Valley Ho was rescued from sure destruction in 2003 and restored to the previous grandeur that attracted the likes of Marilyn Monroe, Humphrey Bogart, and Zsa Zsa Gabor back in its heyday. While this hotel evokes a Rat Pack–era image, it's decidedly modern. In this ninety-minute tour, you'll discover some of its old charms and new secrets. You'll also hear all about its days as a Hollywood hangout and who got married where.

6850 E Main St., Scottsdale, AZ 85251, 480-248-2000
Hotel Valley Ho

TIP

The tour costs $19.56 (fitting!), and includes discounts for the hotel's spectacular VH Spa and its on-site restaurant, Cafe Zu Zu. For tour information, call the Ultimate Art & Culture Tours at 480-634-6850.

UNIVERSITY OF PHOENIX STADIUM

SPORTS AND RECREATION

WATCH THE CUBBIES PLAY A SPRING TRAINING GAME AT SLOAN PARK

To smell the freshly mown grass, feel the warm Arizona sun on your face, and hear a rousing rendition of "Take Me Out to the Ballgame" when the rest of the country is busy shoveling snow is one of the best gifts Phoenix can give, and the Chicago Cubs are the most-watched team in the Cactus League. The Cubs' new park opened in 2014 as Cubs Park; however, in early 2015 it was renamed Sloan Park after the more than one-hundred-year-old Chicago-based Sloan Valve Company. No matter the name, it's still the park that traditionally sells out as baseball fans from all over come to fill the stadium to capacity. And if you're from Chicago, you'll love that they're not only selling hot dogs in the food court, but also mini deep dish Giordano's pizzas.

Cactusleague.com

TIP

There are fourteen other major league teams in the Cactus League, playing at stadiums across the Valley in Tempe, Mesa, Goodyear, Glendale, Phoenix, Peoria, Surprise, and Scottsdale. Be sure to catch a game while you're here. If you're set on catching the Cubs, you'll want to buy tickets in advance. And if you don't want to walk too far, arrive early; general parking is on a first-come, first-served basis. On non–game days, the Cubs can be seen playing on the practice fields from about 9 a.m. until 12:30 p.m.

SNAG A FRONT ROW SEAT
AT THE ARIZONA DIAMONDBACKS' CHASE FIELD

Even in the off-seasons, you can find a seat at Friday's Front Row. The TGI Friday's restaurant is located behind left field at Chase Field where the Arizona Diamondbacks play baseball. Open year-round, a quiet lunchtime visit offers a unique view of the baseball diamond. During baseball season, you may even find the D-backs practicing out on the field below. On game days, you can reserve a spot at the restaurant for full service seating with an incredible view. If you have a big group, rent the suite with the private balcony overlooking the field. For smaller groups, try the tables in the 130s; they'll give you the best views on game day. The restaurant also offers bleacher seating during games with full food and beverage service.

401 E Jefferson St,, Phoenix, AZ 85004, 602-462-6500
Frontrowphoenix.com

TIP

To reserve your spot at Friday's Front Row during a D-backs game, call 602-462-3506.

CHEER ON (OR BOO)

YOUR FAVORITE GOLFER ON THE 16TH HOLE AT THE WASTE MANAGEMENT OPEN

Nowhere on the PGA Tour will you find a crowd as rowdy as the one at the 16th hole at the annual Phoenix Waste Management Open at TPC Scottsdale. The only fully enclosed hole on any course, it's one of the loudest and most entertaining holes in golf—for players and fans alike. No pressure for the golfers, but they will not find any polite golf claps here. Instead, the more than fifteen thousand fans filling the seats around this par 3 are probably the rowdiest in golf history, and they're encouraged to cheer for the good and boo for the bad. And they do so enthusiastically. Every year the noise gets a little louder as they add more and more seats to the stadium seating, but it's all for a good cause. The Open, which was started in 1932 by the Phoenix Thunderbirds, has raised almost $100 million to date for Phoenix charities. If you're hoping to witness a little golf history, you better arrive early. Unless you know someone in the sponsorship boxes and suites, you may miss out. The seats on the 16th hole are first-come, first-served, and they go fast.

17020 N Hayden Rd., Scottsdale, AZ 85255, 480-585-4334
Wmphoenixopen.com

TEE OFF
AT TROON NORTH

For a challenging course and an outstanding view, consider one of Troon North Golf Club's two award-winning courses—Pinnacle and Monument. Designed by British Open champion Tom Weiskopf, Troon North is located in the hills of Pinnacle Peak in north Scottsdale, above the valley floor. Its pristine lawns, rugged mountain vistas, and majestic saguaro cacti offer a picturesque setting. Pair the stunning view with the desert challenges, like deep ravines, quarries, granite boulders, sandy washes, and hidden greens—not to mention the sand traps of a traditional course—and you'll find a challenging game of golf. Not that it's any consolation, but even if your golf game is less than stellar, the views from the tee box and along the course are still memorable.

10320 E Dynamite Blvd., Scottsdale, AZ 85262, 480-585-5300
Troonnorthgolf.com

TIP

If you love golf, the Valley offers a number of public and semiprivate courses. Your best bet may be the resort courses such as those at the Arizona Biltmore, the Phoencian, and the Westin Kierland.

CHEER ON
THE ASU SUN DEVILS

If you're an NCAA basketball or football fan, then you may have seen the ASU Sun Devils make history within the walls of Wells Fargo Arena and Sun Devil Stadium (aka Frank Kush Field), respectively. Watch a game live at either of these venues. You may recall that Sun Devil Stadium is where the Arizona Cardinals played NFL football from the late 1980s until they moved to University of Phoenix Stadium in 2006. It's also where President Barak Obama spoke at ASU's commencement ceremonies in 2009. In 2014, the university started a fundraising drive to rebuild the stadium, so get in a visit before it changes. In addition to basketball and football, you may want to catch Sun Devils baseball and women's basketball and softball. There are over twenty men's and women's collegiate sports at ASU.

Sun Devil Ticket Office, single-game tickets, 480-727-0000
Toll-Free, 888-786-3857, Thesundevils.com

86

TOUR UNIVERSITY OF PHOENIX STADIUM

WHERE THE ARIZONA CARDINALS PLAY

Truly an amazing feat of technology, architecture, and urban design, University of Phoenix Stadium is the only stadium in the U.S. with both a retractable roof and a roll-out playing field. Designed to incorporate and reflect the features of the Sonoran Desert upon which it was built, you'll discover firsthand that the light of the setting sun plays off the outer panels of the stadium, the twenty-one vertical glass panels reveal the desert vistas, and the translucent "Bird-Air" fabric roof invites the beautiful desert climate in even when the roof is closed. You'll also discover lots of fun facts about the stadium, like the fact that its outer skin is reminiscent of a barrel cactus, and that the tray the grass field rolls out on weighs almost nineteen million pounds.

1 Cardinals Dr., Glendale, AZ 85305, 623-433-7101
Universityofphoenixstadium.com

TIP

Tours happen most Thursdays through Sundays, but double-check the calendar. They post tour dates about two months in advance. Reserve your tickets ahead of time.

WALK, BIKE, OR RUN
THE TRAILS BESIDE THE SCENIC ARIZONA CANALS

Water in the desert is something to celebrate, and many of the canals in the Phoenix area have been lovingly landscaped to entice both locals and tourists to enjoy these areas. Built on abandoned irrigation ditches built by the original settlers of the Salt River Valley—the Hohokam—the Valley's canal system is quite extensive. The canals and their running/biking trails stretch for miles through neighborhoods and across city streets and city boundaries. Two of the best canal paths can be found in Tempe and in the Biltmore area of Phoenix. The Western Canal begins in Tempe at Kiwanis Park on Baseline Road and runs south of Guadalupe Road through Ken MacDonald Golf Course where it turns east toward Mesa. The Arizona Canal between 40th and 24th Streets north of Camelback Road takes you below the historic Wrigley Mansion and alongside the Arizona Biltmore Resort and golf course.

Srpnet.com/water/canals/distances.aspx

TIP

You can only bike, walk, or run along the canals; no motorized vehicles are allowed. Some of the paths are paved, but many are unpaved.

88

HEAD TO THE TOP
OF PIESTEWA PEAK FOR A 360-DEGREE VIEW

If you're the kind of person who wants to earn that 360-degree view of Phoenix under your own power, then a hike to the summit of Piestewa Peak should be on your to-do list. The stair-like climb will take you to an elevation of about twenty-six hundred feet above the desert floor. Take your time, pause as you climb to take in the sights. As you climb, directly below you to the south will be the Wrigley Mansion (of the Wrigley Field Wrigleys—this was once their winter home), and south of that is the well-known and historic Arizona Biltmore and its two PGA golf courses. In the distance to the south you'll see downtown Phoenix and Chase Field. Once you scramble those last few feet to the top, take a breather, and then turn, turn, keep turning, and savor that view (trust me, you will have earned it).

2701 E Squaw Peak Dr., Phoenix, AZ 85016, 602-261-8318

TIP

The earlier in the day you hit the trail the better. Parking is easier to find and the trail is often crowded later in the day. Also, don't do a double-take, chances are that runner passing you on the trail has already passed you once. Many local runners train on the steep summit climb. Don't worry about getting lapped; it's not a race.

MOUNTAIN BIKE
THROUGH THE COUNTRY'S LARGEST CITY PARK

As the direct result of FDR's Emergency Conservation Act, the men of what would later become the Civilian Conservation Corps built more than forty miles of trail between 1933 and 1940. Today, the Phoenix South Mountain Preserve at sixteen thousand acres in south Phoenix is actually the largest city park in the United States. Criss-crossed with more than fifty miles of trail with several entry points in and around the city, the park offers trails to meet just about every athletic capability—from a leisurely walk to a rugged climb. It's especially fun for mountain biking as there are wide, flat trails like the 9-mile Desert Classic Trail that skirts around the south side of the mountains as well as the shorter 1.2 mile Mormon Trail, which is more technical and challenging.

TIP

While the parking lots and roadways around the entry points tend to get pretty crowded early in the day, the crowd quickly thins out across the sixteen thousand acres and you may not see another hiker or biker until you head back to the trailhead.

REI at Priest and Southern along the Tempe-Phoenix border offers some of the best hiking and biking maps in the area. Pick up one of the South Mountain for a look at the various trailheads, entry points, and elevation changes.

Main Entrance Address: 10919 S Central Ave., 85042
Pima Canyon Entrance: 9904 S 48th St., 85044
602-262-7393
Phoenix.gov/parks/trails/locations/south-mountain

CATCH THE CITY VIEW
FROM CAMELBACK MOUNTAIN

One of the most popular hikes in the Valley, Camelback has two different routes to the summit. The Echo Canyon Summit Trail, which is often so crowded during tourist season (not the summer) that cars wait in line to get into the parking lot. The Summit Trail is only about 1.2 miles; however, it's almost a thirten-hundred-foot elevation change, which means it's a fairly steep climb and the trail is narrow in places. For a less crowded hike, you can try the lesser-known Cholla Trail. It's a little longer at just under 1.5 miles, but offers a more gradual climb. The views from either trail are equally spectacular. As you climb, you'll notice the multimillion dollar homes dotting the mountainsides, and the Valley spreading out before you.

4925 E McDonald Dr., 602-261-8318
www.phoenix.gov/parks/trails/locations/camelback-mountain

TIP

Don't underestimate the dry desert weather. Bring plenty of water when you hike. Don't forget the hat and sunscreen either. The Cholla Trail begins at Cholla Lane off 64th Street/Invergordon in a residential neighborhood. You can get to Echo Canyon off McDonald Drive east of Tatum. Camelback is named for its resemblance to a reclining camel. Both hikes can be accessed off Camelback Road between Scottsdale Road and 44th Street.

HISTORIC
THE
HANDLEBAR
Tempe
MILL AVE
COMMERCIAL LOADING ZONE
NO BICYCLING OR SKATEBOARDING ON SIDEWALK
TAXI STANDING

SHOPPING AND FASHION

ENJOY ARIZONA'S
OPEN-AIR SHOPPING EXPERIENCES

Chief among Arizona's outdoor malls may be Biltmore Fashion Park, located in the upscale Camelback Corridor at the corner of 24th Street and Camelback. The Biltmore shopping area provides a blend of big stores like Macy's and Saks Fifth Avenue with retail outfitters like Ralph Lauren, White House/Black Market, and The Limited; big brands like Apple and Williams-Sonoma; local retailers such as Queen Creek Olive Mill Oils & Olives; and national and local restaurants such as the Cheesecake Factory, Short Leash Hot Dogs, Zinburger, and Stingray Sushi. If you're a fan of the outdoor shopping experience, you can also try Tempe Marketplace in Tempe, Kierland Commons in north Phoenix, Westgate Entertainment District in Glendale, or San Tan Village in Gilbert. Each offers a blend of local and national stores and restaurants.

2502 E Camelback Rd., Phoenix, AZ 85016, 602-955-8400
Shopbiltmore.com

2000 E Rio Salado Pkwy., Tempe, AZ 85281, 480-966-9338
Tempemarketplace.com

15205 N Kierland Blvd., Scottsdale, AZ 85254, 480-348-1577
Kierlandcommons.com

6751 N Sunset Blvd., Glendale, AZ 85305, 623-385-7502
Westgateaz.com

2218 E Williams Field Rd., Ste. 235, Gilbert, AZ 8529, 480-282-9500
Shopsantanvillage.com

MEET THE AUTHOR
AT CHANGING HANDS BOOKSTORE

Book signings, workshops, and talks by authors of local, national, and international acclaim are regular events at this modest store—a local legend among booklovers since 1974—tucked into a strip mall in south Tempe. Over the years, Changing Hands Bookstore has showcased more than a few *New York Times* bestselling authors, from Clive Cussler and President Barack Obama (when he was still a senator from Chicago), to celebrity authors like Ozzy Osbourne, and local superstars like Jana Bommersbach and Betty Webb. On top of the top-notch illustrators and authors lined up to share their passion for their craft, the store is packed with both new and used books, gifts and novelty items, and staff members who can make great book recommendations for new readers to early readers and beyond.

Tempe Square Shopping Center
6428 S McClintock Dr., Tempe, AZ, 480-730-0205
Phoenix, 300 W Camelback Rd. Phoenix, AZ, 602-274-0067
www.changinghands.com

TIP

Browse their website or pick up their monthly newsletter to find out who is in store this week. Changing Hands hosts events geared toward families, young adult and teen readers, as well as adults.

BUY LOCALLY
AT THE FARMERS' MARKETS

Despite its desert setting, Phoenix and its surrounding areas support a number of small farms and local growers and plenty of local retailers, bakers, artists, salsa makers, and more who sell their food, arts, and crafts at the weekly local farmers' markets across the Valley. Among the best to visit on Saturdays is the Scottsdale Farmers' Market in Old Town Scottsdale at 1st and Brown and the Open Air Market adjacent to the Phoenix Public Market Cafe at 1st and Pierce in downtown Phoenix. Locals head to markets in Tempe, Gilbert, Mesa, Carefree, Sun City, Anthem, and Ahwatukee to find local vendors selling everything from soaps, lotions, wood-turning objet d'art, honey, tortillas, and tamales to music, arts, and crafts. Due to the heat, many of these farmers' markets adjust their hours or close for the summer. The Open Air Market in downtown Phoenix is open every Saturday year-round.

721 N Central Ave. (Central and McKinley), 602-625-6736
Arizonacommunityfarmersmarkets.com, Phxpublicmarket.com

94

DISCOVER UNIQUE FINDS
AT THESE VALLEY GIFT SHOPS

If you're looking for something exceptional to take back home, consider these four Valley gift shops: the Museum Store at the Phoenix Art Museum sells a plethora of one-of-a-kind items, many of them inspired by art or artists in its collection. It also features works from local artists. The Heard Museum, Phoenix's Native American museum, features authentic Native American art and purchases most of its inventory directly from the artists themselves, including books, paintings, pottery, sculptures, jewelry, and weavings by American Indian authors and artists. Another great place to pick up Arizona- and Southwest-inspired gifts is the Arizona Highways Gift Shop, located at the magazine's offices in a quiet westside Phoenix neighborhood at 2039 West Lewis. You can also discover unique music-inspired finds at the Museum Store at the Musical Instrument Museum in north Scottsdale.

The Museum Store at the Phoenix Art Museum, 1625 N Central Ave.
Phoenix, AZ 85004, 602-257-1222, Phxart.org/store

Heard Museum Shop, 2301 N Central Ave., Phoenix, AZ 85004
602-252-8840, Heardmuseumshop.com

Arizona Highways Gift Shop, 2039 W Lewis Ave., Phoenix, AZ 85009
602-712-2200, Shoparizonahighways.com

Musical Instrument Museum, 4725 E Mayo Blvd., Phoenix, AZ 85050
480-478-6000, MIM.org/museum-store

95

STROLL
THROUGH HISTORIC GLENDALE

Comprised of two historic neighborhoods—Caitlin Court and Old Town—historic downtown Glendale features a blend of Caitlin Court's bungalow-style shops and white picket fences and Old Town's gaslamp-lit, tree-lined corridors and antique shops. Spread out across ten blocks in the heart of Glendale, the area is loaded with shops, boutiques, and craft makers as well as restaurants, pubs, ethnic eateries, and coffee shops. Take your time wandering along the avenues and in and out of the stores. The array of shops includes antique stores; a toy and model train shop; garden and home decor retailers; vintage shops with one-of-a-kind collectibles, hand-crafted gifts, and jewelry; tarot card readers; a furniture store; gift shops; a comic store; a clockmaker; bakeries; and even a chocolate maker—the Cerreta Candy Company.

Murphy Park, 58th and Glendale Avenues, Historic Downtown Glendale
Visitglendale.com

TIP

One local restaurant favorite is Mexican restaurant Bitz-ee Mama's, whose large and delicious breakfast menu attracts die-hard fans from across the Valley. Another longtime favorite is A Touch of European Cafe—located in one of those historic bungalows—where you'll find fresh pierogi (delicious Polish dumplings).

INDULGE YOUR SENSES
WITH AN UBER-RELAXING SPA TREATMENT

The Phoenix and Scottsdale areas abound with resorts widely renowned for their spas, each with its own style and personality. Booking one of their sixty- to ninety-minute treatments will leave you feeling relaxed and refreshed for another hike up Camelback Mountain, another round of golf, or a second bike across the desert at South Mountain Park Preserve. Depending on your taste and style, you'll find something to fit your fancy. Find a Mediterranean-inspired citrus grove facial at Alvadora Spa at the Royal Palms, a pineapple-infused South Pacific Vichy body polish at Jurelique at FireSky Resort & Spa, a desert-based agave enchantment massage at Agave Spa at the Westin Kierland, or a Native American–influenced Pima medicine massage at Aji Spa at Wild Horse Pass Resort & Spa. (And these are just a few of my favorite things.)

SADDLE UP
AT THE COWBOY SHOPS IN OLD TOWN SCOTTSDALE

Old Town Scottsdale sports its share of shops hawking everything from Western wear—think cowboy hats, cowboy boots, and leather goods to cowboy art and Native American artistry and all the novelty items in between. Stop by any number of these local shops to pick out a piece of Arizona to take back home. Be sure to pick up your cowboy boots or cowboy hat so you'll fit right in at places like HandlebarJ's and the Rusty Spur. For a one-stop shop, try Bischoff's Shades of the West where you'll find all sorts of gear, gifts, and Southwest-themed goods from burn-your-lips-off hot sauce to high-end Western wear.

7247 E Main St., Scottsdale, AZ 85251, 480-945-3289
shadesofthewest.com

TIP

Wander over to the gallery at Bischoff's at the Park, located at the western edge of Civic Park Plaza on Brown, for a look at works (sculptures, pottery, fine art) by artists from the West and Southwest as well as artists representing several Native American tribes like the Navajo.

3925 N Brown Ave., Scottsdale, AZ 85251
480-946-6155, bischoffsouthwestart.com

98

DISCOVER
DOWNTOWN TEMPE

The Downtown Tempe Authority, responsible for building a thriving city center, says it best on their website: "Look around and look up to see Tempe rising." And Tempe is rising, turning into an urban oasis in the middle of metropolitan Phoenix. What was once considered the Mill Avenue Entertainment District is now a sprawling stretch of more than one hundred music venues, restaurants, shops, and boutiques extending well beyond Mill. After a series of evolutions from hippie hangouts and indie shops to big-brand stores and chain restaurants, downtown Tempe is finally settling into a beautiful blend of local retailers, favorite brand stores, and one-of-a-kind boutiques. Park in the parking garage off Ash or grab a metered spot and stroll along the tree-lined streets. You'll find fun shops like the Candy Addict, which carries just about every '80s kid's favorite childhood candy, and the perfect hippie place to shop at Hippie Gypsy.

FEED YOUR PASSION
FOR FASHION AT SCOTTSDALE FASHION SQUARE

If you're a fashionista of any kind, then a stop at Scottsdale Fashion Square at Scottsdale and Camelback Roads is a must for you. This upscale, multilevel indoor shopping mall is perfect during the hot summer months and highlights some of the biggest names and hottest trends in fashion. Let's start with high-end anchor stores like Barneys New York, Neiman Marcus, and Nordstrom and work our way in toward retail space for fashion designers like Ted Baker, Michael Kors, and Jimmy Choo. And then, of course, you'll find all the traditional favorites like Fossil, J. Crew, and Ann Taylor. Like the Musical Instrument Museum, you may want to schedule time to come back, because chances are you won't hit every shop in one day.

Scottsdale Fashion Square
7014 E Camelback Rd., #2020, Scottsdale, AZ 85251, 480-423-6943
Fashionsquare.com

TIP

For another great indoor mall, try Chandler Fashion Center off Loop 101 and Chandler Boulevard.

SHOP
DOWNTOWN CHANDLER

With the historic San Marcos Resort as its centerpiece, downtown Chandler, concentrated along Arizona Avenue between Chandler Road and Frye Boulevard, has become a fun and charming shopping, dining, and entertainment district in the suburban sprawl of metropolitan Phoenix. This on-the-rise area boasts local specialty shops like Sibley's West, which features local artists, Arizona books, art, wine, and goods. You can make your own pottery and art at Burst of Butterflies, find cowboy attire at Saba's Western Wear, and buy women's clothing and accessories at One Wing Boutique. As afternoon wanes into evening, laughter and the fragrances of good food spill out onto the lantern-lit sidewalks. Come for an afternoon of shopping and browsing and stay for a beer at San Tan Brewery, or a glass of wine at Vintage 95, and maybe dinner and some live music at El Zocalo Mexican Grill.

Arizona Avenue between Buffalo and Boston Streets
Downtownchandler.com

TIP

For a unique twist on an old standard—coffee—try Peixoto (pronounced pay-SHOW-tow) Coffee. The Brazilian-inspired, family-owned coffee lounge located just south of Boston on Arizona Avenue features a nitro cold brew—a delicious glass of cold brew coffee on tap, complete with beer-like foam. It looks oddly like a small glass of Guinness. Try the nitro float—the cold brew coffee with a dollop of ice cream.

SUGGESTED ITINERARIES

ARCHITECTURE

DATE NIGHT

DISCOVER THE DESERT

FAMILY-FRIENDLY

FOODIE FUN

FREE ACTIVITIES

COWBOY CULTURE

NATIVE AMERICAN

OUTDOOR ACTIVITIES

GUIDED TOURS

ACTIVITIES BY SEASON

WINTER

Celebrate the Season with Lights, 62

Encounter Arizona's Native American Cultures with Native Trails, 86

Witness the World Championship Hoop Dance Contest, 87

Cheer on (or Boo) Your Favorite Golfer on the 16th Hole at the Waste Management Open, 113

Sample Your Way through the Annual Chocolate Affaire in Glendale, 56

Attend the Annual Greater Phoenix Jewish Film Festival, 98

Discover Phoenix's Historic Districts, 100

SPRING

Encounter Arizona's Native American Cultures with Native Trails, 86

Watch the Cubbies Play a Spring Training Game at Sloan Park, 110

Listen to Live Music Friday Nights at the Desert Botanical Garden, 61

Watch Wide-Eyed as the Fighter Jets Fly by at the Luke Days Air Show, 80

Watch the Desert Come Alive in March at Boyce Thompson Arboretum, 43

Hike, Slide, Swim, Climb, and Rappel Your Way through Salome Canyon, 29

SUMMER

FALL

INDEX